A Scandal in Bohemia

SIR ARTHUR CONAN DOYLE

Level 3

Retold by Ronald Holt
Series Editors: Andy Hopkins and Jocelyn Potter

Pearson Education Limited

Edinburgh Gate, Harlow,
Essex CM20 2JE, England
and Associated Companies throughout the world.

ISBN: 978-1-4058-6233-2

First published in the Longman Structural Readers Series 1976
This adaptation first published by Addison Wesley Longman Limited
in the Longman Fiction Series 1996
First published by Penguin Books 1999
This edition published 2008

3 5 7 9 10 8 6 4

Original copyright © The Copyright holders of the Sir Arthur Conan Doyle
works, reproduced by kind permission of Jonathan Clowes Ltd London,
on behalf of Andrea Plunket, Trustee & Administrator
Text copyright © Penguin Books Ltd 1999
This edition copyright © Pearson Education Ltd 2008
Illustrations by Linda Clark

Typeset by Graphicraft Ltd, Hong Kong
Set in 11/14pt Bembo
Printed in China
SWTC/03

Published by Pearson Education Ltd in association with
Penguin Books Ltd, both companies being subsidiaries of Pearson Plc

For a complete list of the titles available in the Penguin Readers series please write to your local
Pearson Longman office or to: Penguin Readers Marketing Department, Pearson Education,
Edinburgh Gate, Harlow, Essex CM20 2JE, England.

Contents

Introduction

'What does a woman do if there is a fire? She tries to save her most important things. A married woman saves her baby. An unmarried woman saves her gold and silver. Now what was most important to our lady?'

As usual in a Sherlock Holmes story, Dr Watson, the detective's good friend and helper, has not noticed small but very important facts in the case. So Sherlock Holmes explains to Watson – and to us – how he has solved the mystery. The great detective understands how men and women act. He knows what the lady in 'A Scandal in Bohemia' will save from a fire in her house. He also notices the shape of a shoe or a man's dirty trousers. We start every story like Dr Watson – we do not know anything. We are not as quick to understand as Holmes. But soon we learn the facts, and then Sherlock Holmes guides us through the case. It is exciting to understand the criminal's mind. It is even more exciting to understand Sherlock Holmes's way of working. When he gets inside a criminal mind, he solves the mystery.

Arthur Conan Doyle was born on 22 May 1859 in Edinburgh, the capital of Scotland. He came from an Irish-Catholic family, and almost all of his relatives were successful in some way – but not his father. Charles Doyle drank too much, and so the children listened to their mother. Mary Doyle loved books and had a gift for story-telling. Her voice brought stories to life for young Arthur.

After his ninth birthday, Arthur went to school in England and stayed there for seven years. At first he felt very sad and lonely, but a few things made him happy. He loved to write letters to his mother and to receive letters from her. He enjoyed sports and was very good at most ball games. He also realised that he had his mother's gift for story-telling. He often had a crowd of boys around him, listening to his interesting and amusing stories.

This was good preparation for his life as a writer. But before Arthur Conan Doyle started to write, he studied medicine at the University of Edinburgh. One of the most important people in this part of his life was a teacher, Dr Joseph Bell. Bell stayed in Arthur's memory because of his great intelligence, his careful examination of facts and his way of explaining things clearly. Doyle was thinking of Dr Bell when he began to write about Sherlock Holmes.

Doyle became a doctor, but his business was never very successful. Because he did not have a lot of patients, he had time for writing. One of his stories was printed in *Chambers's Edinburgh Journal* before he was twenty years old. In 1887, when he was twenty-eight, he introduced Holmes, the great detective, in his first important work, 'A Study in Scarlet'. Very soon both Doyle and Holmes were famous.

Arthur Conan Doyle was very happy with the success of his Sherlock Holmes stories and books, and in 1890 he became a full-time writer. During his life, he wrote four books and fifty-six stories with Sherlock Holmes at the centre of mysterious and interesting detective cases. Most of these works first came out in *The Strand*, a popular magazine.

But Doyle had many interests and he grew tired of Sherlock Holmes and the popularity of his adventures. In 1893 he surprised the world by killing Holmes and his greatest enemy, Dr Moriarty, in 'The Final Problem'. Immediately, 20,000 *Strand* readers refused to buy another copy of the magazine.

Now Doyle had time to write other types of mystery and adventure stories. His science fiction books with Professor Challenger at the centre also became very popular. But even more important to Doyle than literature were his factual books about war. At the start of the second Boer War (1899–1902), Doyle was too old to be a soldier, but he went to war as a doctor. After the war he wrote *The Great Boer War*, an intelligent look at wartime activities. In 1902, King Edward VII made him *Sir* Arthur Conan Doyle because of his wartime help to his country. Before the First World War (1914–18), Doyle sent ideas and suggestions to the government. Sadly, one of his sons, his brother and other close relatives were killed in that war.

Doyle wrote many other books. But he realised that Sherlock Holmes could not stay dead. His readers loved the detective too much for that, and Doyle needed money. One of his most famous Sherlock Holmes books, *The Hound of the Baskervilles*, was written in 1901. Then, in 1903, he wrote 'The Return of Sherlock Holmes'. Doyle still had other interests – politics, sport, travel, fast cars and his family – but Sherlock Holmes stayed with him until the end. Doyle died on 7 July 1930 with his second wife and family at his bedside.

To Sir Arthur Conan Doyle, Sherlock Holmes was a fictional detective, but to people in many countries he was more than that. He continues to be one of the most famous people in English literature. Today's readers enjoy listening to Dr Watson as he tells the stories of Sherlock Holmes's adventures. The stories are now studied at universities, and there are many Sherlock Holmes clubs around the world. Arthur Conan Doyle's great detective is also still alive at cinemas and on television. The first Sherlock Holmes film was made in 1917, and there is a new film or television programme about the great detective almost every year.

A Scandal in Bohemia

Only one person ever beat Sherlock Holmes. Irene Adler was that person and Holmes never forgot her.

I was not seeing much of Holmes in those days. After my marriage I moved to another part of London, while Holmes stayed in our Baker Street rooms. I was also working very hard as a doctor, so I did not often have time to visit him.

But one night in March 1888 I was returning home from a visit to a sick woman. As I passed my old rooms, I looked up. There was a light in Holmes's room and I could see him at work there. He was standing with his hands behind his back and his head down. He was clearly thinking about a new problem. What was he working on now? I decided to visit him and find out.

Holmes was standing by the fire, thinking deeply. He did not say anything, so I just sat down. Holmes was always like this when he was thinking about a problem. But I think he was pleased to see me. Finally he picked up a piece of paper. 'Look at this, Watson,' he said. 'What do you think about this?'

I took the paper. It was a note. There was no address, there was no date and it was not signed.

'A man will visit you tonight at a quarter to eight,' the note said. 'Do not be surprised if he is wearing a mask. He will not tell you his real name. He needs your help with a very important problem. Please do not tell anyone about his visit.'

'This is a mystery,' I said. 'What does it mean, Holmes?'

'We shall soon see,' Holmes answered, looking out of the window. 'A carriage has just stopped at our door. It's a beautiful carriage. Our visitor is an important man.'

A few moments later we heard footsteps outside the door.

'Come in!' called Holmes.

1

The man who came in was very tall. He was wearing a mask and his clothes looked foreign.

'Did you receive my note?' he asked. He sounded German to me.

'Yes,' Holmes replied. 'Please sit down. This is my friend Dr Watson. Your note was not signed. Would you tell me your name?'

'You can call me Count von Kramm. I am from Bohemia. I have come to ask for your help. But you must not tell anyone about my visit. It has to stay a secret, at the request of a King. Can I talk freely in front of your friend?'

'Of course,' answered Holmes. 'Dr Watson often helps me with my work. You can speak freely. You are in fact the King, are you not?'

The man jumped from his chair and pulled the mask from his face. 'You are quite right,' he cried. 'I am the King of Bohemia. How did you know?'

'It was quite easy,' said Holmes. 'You have a beautiful carriage with two beautiful horses. You are a rich man. It is clear that you are a very important man.'

'But that does not explain . . .'

'You have come to ask for my help,' continued Holmes. 'You say that I must not tell anyone about your visit. You talk about the request of a King . . . You are from Bohemia. I have read in the newspapers that the King of Bohemia is in London at the moment. So I know that you are the King. Please tell me what I can do for you.'

'These are the facts,' began the King. 'About five years ago I met a lady named Irene Adler. Perhaps her name means something to you?'

'I will look at my notes,' said Holmes. He went to a case which was full of cards. There were notes about hundreds of people on the cards. After a few moments he pulled out a card. 'Irene Adler,' he read. 'Born in New Jersey in 1858. A singer.

The man jumped from his chair and pulled the mask from his face.

La Scala and Warsaw. Now living in London.'

He turned to the King.

'Five years ago, Irene Adler was living in Warsaw. Did you meet her there?'

'Yes,' said the King.

'You fell in love and wrote some letters to her. Now you want the lady to return the letters.'

'Yes. But how . . . ?'

'Was there a secret marriage?'

'No.'

'Did you sign anything . . . any papers?'

'None.'

'Then there is no problem.'

'But the letters . . .'

'You can say that you did not write them.'

'She has a photograph,' said the King sadly.

'Perhaps she bought it.'

'But we are both in the photograph.'

'Oh!' said Holmes. 'That is different. You will have to buy the photograph from her.'

'I tried to do that, but she refuses to sell it.'

'Steal it then.'

'Twice I paid men to steal it but they could not find the photograph in her house.'

Holmes laughed. 'We have quite a problem,' he said. 'What is the lady going to do with the photograph?'

'The King of Scandinavia has a daughter. I am going to marry her. Irene Adler is going to use the photograph to stop the marriage.'

'I heard that you were going to be married,' said Holmes. 'How is Irene Adler going to stop you?'

'She will send the photograph to the King of Scandinavia. He is afraid of any scandal and will stop the marriage.'

4

'And why doesn't Irene Adler want you to marry the King's daughter?'

'It is the usual reason. She is in love with me and she wants me to marry her.'

'Are you sure that the photograph is not already on its way to Scandinavia?'

'I am sure.'

'Why?'

'She is waiting until they print the date of my wedding in the newspapers. That will be next Monday. She will then send the photograph to the King.'

'Then we have three more days,' said Holmes. 'Are you staying in London?'

'Of course. I am staying at the Langham Hotel.'

'Then I shall write to you there. I shall soon have some news for you. Now, the question of money.'

'You can name your own price,' said the King. 'I will give anything to get that photograph.'

'I shall need some money now,' said Holmes. 'I shall have to pay for some help.'

The King took some notes from his pocket and counted them. 'There is a thousand pounds,' he said. 'I hope that will be enough.'

Holmes took the money. 'What is the lady's address?' he asked.

'Briony Lodge, Serpentine Avenue, St John's Wood.'

Holmes made a note of it. 'One more question,' he said. 'How big is the photograph?'

'It's quite large. It's about twelve inches by eight.'

'Then good night. I shall have some news for you very soon. And good night, Watson,' he added, after the King closed the door. 'Will you come to see me tomorrow afternoon at three o'clock? I would like your help.'

◆

The next afternoon at three o'clock I went to Baker Street. Holmes was not there, so I waited for him. It was four o'clock when the door opened. The man who came in was dressed as a carriage driver. His hair was long and his face was red. It was Holmes! Without saying a word he went into his bedroom. Five minutes later he came out. His hair was short, his face was clean and he was wearing his usual clothes.

He sat near the fire and laughed. 'Well, Watson,' he said. 'How do you think I spent the day?'

'Let me think . . . You were watching Irene Adler's house.'

'Yes, I was. I left here at eight o'clock this morning dressed as a driver. I soon found Briony Lodge. It is a large house with a garden at the back. The front of the house is on the road. At the side of the house there are some buildings for carriages and horses. I found a driver there who told me all about Irene Adler.'

'What did he tell you?' I asked.

'She is very beautiful. She lives quietly and sings at concerts. She goes for a drive every day at five o'clock and always returns at seven o'clock for dinner. Only one man visits her. He is dark and good-looking. He goes to the house every day. His name is Godfrey Norton and he is a lawyer.'

'You had a busy day,' I said.

'That is not all,' Holmes continued. 'This Godfrey Norton is very important. Why is a lawyer visiting Irene Adler every day? Is he just her lawyer or is he a friend? Is he in love with her? If he is just her lawyer, perhaps he is keeping the photograph for her. If they are in love, perhaps she does not want him to see it; then it is possible that the photograph is in her house. While I was there, a carriage drove up to Briony Lodge. A dark, good-looking man jumped out. It was clearly Godfrey Norton and he seemed to be in a great hurry. He shouted to the driver to wait and then he ran into the house.

'He stayed there for about half an hour. I could see him through the sitting-room window, but I could not see the woman. Godfrey Norton seemed to be very excited. Then he came out of the house, ran to the carriage and looked at his watch. "Take me to Regent Street. I have to buy a ring. Then take me to the Church of St Monica in the Edgware Road," he shouted to the driver. "I'll give you a pound if you get there in twenty minutes."

'The carriage left,' Holmes continued. 'Then Irene Adler's own carriage came to the front of the house. Irene Adler came out of the house and got into the carriage. "The Church of St Monica, John," she cried. The carriage left. I decided to follow her. A carriage drove past and I jumped into it. I arrived at the church and hurried inside. There was nobody there except Irene Adler, Godfrey Norton and a priest. When I came in, they all looked at me. Godfrey Norton ran over to me. "Come with me," he cried. "We need a witness. It won't take long. Only a few minutes." He then pulled me to the front of the church. There I was, a witness at the wedding of Irene Adler and Godfrey Norton. It did not take long. The man thanked me and the woman gave me a pound. The priest smiled. When I think about it, I have to laugh. They could not marry without a witness, so Sherlock Holmes was their witness.'

'So they are married,' I said. 'They seemed to be in a great hurry. What was the reason for that?'

'I think that Irene Adler is afraid,' replied Holmes thoughtfully. 'Someone already tried to steal the photograph twice. I think that she decided to marry Norton and to leave England.'

'Surely the King won't hurt her?' I asked.

'I don't know,' said Holmes. 'But she seems to be afraid of him.'

'What did you do after you left the church?' I asked.

7

'Well,' said Holmes. 'I thought that they were going to leave London. I was very surprised when I heard the woman say to Norton, "I shall drive to the park at five as usual." They left in different carriages. Now I have to move quickly. Will you help me, Watson?'

'Of course,' I said. 'What do you want me to do?'

'It is nearly five o'clock now,' Holmes said. 'In two hours we shall be at Briony Lodge. The woman returns from her drive at seven and we will be there to meet her.'

'And what then?'

'You will see something which will surprise you. But you must not do anything at first. Is that clear? Four or five minutes later, the sitting-room window will open. I want you to stand by that window.'

'And then?'

'Watch me. You will be able to see me. When I lift my hand . . . like this . . . I want you to throw something into the room. Then you will shout "Fire . . . Fire!" '

'Is that all?' I asked.

'Yes,' said Holmes. 'You will throw this into the room.' He picked something up. It was made of metal and about 6 inches long. 'It's a smoke bomb.'

'A smoke bomb!' I cried. 'Is it dangerous?'

'Not at all,' smiled Holmes. 'It will make a lot of smoke. That is all. After you throw it, go to the end of the street. Wait for me there.'

Holmes went into his bedroom. When he came out, he was dressed as a priest. It was a quarter past six when we left Baker Street. We arrived in Serpentine Avenue at ten minutes to seven. It was getting dark while we waited near Briony Lodge. I was surprised to see a lot of people there. Some men were standing near the house. Two policemen were talking to a girl. Some more men were at the corner of the street.

At seven o'clock, Irene Adler's carriage came into the street. It drove to the door of Briony Lodge. While it was stopping, a man ran towards it. He was clearly going to open the door of the carriage, but one of the policemen pushed him away. A fight started. The second policeman and the other men joined in. Irene Adler was now in the middle of a crowd of fighting men. Holmes pushed into the crowd to help her. When he reached her, he gave a loud cry. He fell to the ground; blood was running down his face. The fighting stopped and the fighters ran away. The men who were standing at the corner of the street came to help Holmes.

'How is he?' cried Irene Adler.

'He's dead,' someone said.

'No, he isn't,' said another. 'But he's dying.'

'He's a good man,' said the girl who was talking to the policemen earlier. 'They were going to steal this lady's bag. He stopped them. Ah, he's not dead. But he can't lie in the street.' She looked at Irene Adler. 'Can we bring him into the house?'

'Of course,' she answered. 'Bring him into the sitting room. This way, please.'

Slowly they carried the old priest into Briony Lodge and into the sitting room. I went to the window. From there I could see Holmes lying in a chair. I remembered his orders and took the smoke bomb from my pocket. Holmes sat up and said something to Irene Adler. The woman hurried to the window and opened it. Holmes then lifted his arm. I threw the smoke bomb into the room and shouted 'Fire!' The crowd outside also shouted 'Fire!' I then went to the corner of the street and minutes later Holmes arrived. We started to walk towards Baker Street.

'You did very well, Watson,' he said. 'The result was excellent.'

'Have you got the photograph?'

'I know where it is.'

'And how did you find it?'

9

The men who were standing at the corner of the street came to help Holmes.

'She showed me.'

'Please explain, Holmes.'

'It was quite easy,' he laughed. 'I paid all those people to help me.'

'I thought so.'

'When the fighting started, I ran towards it. Then I fell to the ground. I had some red paint on my hand. I put my hand on my face while I was falling. The red paint looked like blood.'

'Of course.'

'Then they carried me into the house. She had to let me in. What could she do? And into her sitting room. I knew that the photograph was either in there or in her bedroom. They put me in a chair. I asked her to open the window and you had your chance.'

'How did that help you?'

'It was very important. What does a woman do if there is a fire? She tries to save her most important things. A married woman saves her baby. An unmarried woman saves her gold and silver. Now what was most important to our lady? The photograph, of course. It is hidden behind a picture, and she hurried to save it. I saw it when she pulled it out. I then shouted that there was no fire. She put the photograph back, looked at the smoke bomb and ran out of the room. I don't know where she is now. I was going to take the photograph but her driver came in. It seemed safer to wait until later.'

'And what now?' I asked.

'Tomorrow we are going to visit the lady. I shall ask the King to come with us. We shall go into the sitting room to wait for her. But when she arrives, we will not be there. The King can take the photograph himself.'

'And what time will you go?'

'At eight o'clock in the morning. She will be in bed. It will be easy to take the photograph. I will send a message to the King now.'

By this time we were back in Baker Street. When we reached the door, someone who was passing said, 'Good night, Mr Sherlock Holmes.'

There were a lot of people in the street at the time. The speaker seemed to be a young man, but he hurried past us.

'I know that voice,' said Holmes thoughtfully. 'Who was it?'

I slept at Baker Street that night. We were eating breakfast when the King of Bohemia rushed into the room.

'Have you really got the photograph?' he cried.

'Not yet,' said Holmes.

'But you hope to get it.'

'I hope so.'

'Come on then,' said the King. 'Let us go. My carriage is at the door.'

A few minutes later we left for Briony Lodge.

'Irene Adler is married,' Holmes told the King.

'Married! When?'

'Yesterday.'

'But who is she married to?'

'To a lawyer named Norton.'

'But she does not love him.'

'I hope that she does.'

'Why is that?'

'Because your wedding will be safe. If she loves Norton, she does not love you. If she does not love you, she will not try to stop your wedding.'

'That's true,' said the King.

The door of Briony Lodge was open. An old woman stood on the steps.

'Mr Sherlock Holmes?' she asked.

'I am Mr Holmes,' agreed my friend.

'Mrs Norton told me that you were going to come. She left this morning with her husband. They are on their way to France.'

'What!' cried Holmes. 'She has left the country?'

'And she will never return.'

'And the photograph?' cried the King. 'Has she taken it?'

'We shall see,' said Holmes. He pushed past the old woman into the sitting room. The King and I followed him. Holmes went to a painting near the door and turned it over. A photograph and a letter were stuck to the back. The photograph was of Irene Adler in evening dress. On the letter were the words 'To Mr Sherlock Holmes'.

My friend opened the letter and we all read it together. It said:

My dear Mr Holmes,

You were very clever. You discovered where the photograph was. I did not know until I saw the smoke bomb. Someone told me that the King was planning to ask for your help. They even gave me your address. But I did not know that the old priest was really you, Mr Holmes. When I left the sitting room, I sent my driver to watch you. Then I put on men's clothes. When you left, I followed you to Baker Street. I had to know if it was really you. I was the person who said good night to you. Then I went to meet my husband.

We decided that we should leave England now. We do not want to fight you, Mr Holmes. If we do, you will win in the end. We know that. The King need not be afraid of the photograph. I will not do anything to stop his marriage. I love a better man than him. The King was very unkind to me. Because I am afraid of him, I shall keep the photograph. While I have it, he will not be able to hurt me again. I am leaving another photograph which he can keep. I am, dear Mr Sherlock Holmes,

Yours,

IRENE NORTON.

'What a woman — oh what a woman!' cried the King of Bohemia. 'She is the right person in so many ways to be a

13

Queen. But she is so far below me – there is such a difference between us.'

'Yes, there seems to be a great difference between you,' said Holmes coldly. 'I am sorry that we did not get the photograph for you.'

'My dear Mr Holmes,' cried the King. 'That is not important. She promised to do nothing. She always keeps her promises. My wedding is safe.'

'I am happy to hear that you can be confident, sir,' said Holmes.

'How can I thank you, Mr Holmes? Will you take this ring?'

'You have something which I would like much more,' said Holmes.

'Please name it.'

Holmes held up the photograph of Irene Adler in evening dress. 'This photograph,' he said.

The King looked very surprised. 'Irene's photograph!' he cried. 'Of course, if you want it.'

'Thank you. Then there is nothing more to do. I will say goodbye then.' Holmes turned away. Perhaps he did not see the hand that the King held out to him. I returned with Holmes to Baker Street.

◆

And so a great scandal almost touched the King of Bohemia, and a woman beat Sherlock Holmes. Before this he often made jokes about the cleverness of women, but he does not laugh about it now.

The Red-Headed League

When I visited my friend Sherlock Holmes one day last autumn, he was talking to a fat man with bright red hair.

'You have come at a good time, Watson,' said Holmes. He turned to the red-headed man. 'Mr Wilson,' he said, 'this is my good friend Dr Watson. He often helps me. Sit down, Watson. I'd like you to hear this story. Mr Wilson, will you please start again?'

The fat man took a newspaper from his pocket and opened it. 'Read that, Dr Watson,' he said.

I took the newspaper and looked at it. The words that were marked were:

To the Red-Headed League. There is now a free place in the League for a man who wants to earn four pounds a week. The League was started by Mr Ezekiah Hopkins of Pennsylvania, USA, who left all his money to it. Only healthy men with red hair can join. If your hair is red, come to 7 Fleet Street on Monday at 11 o'clock. Ask for Mr Duncan Ross.

'What is this Red-Headed League?' I asked.

Holmes laughed. 'Mr Wilson will explain,' he said. 'Look at the newspaper, Watson. What is the date on it?'

I looked at the date on the newspaper. 'It was 27 April 1890,' I replied. 'That's just two months ago.'

'Very good. Please continue your story, Mr Wilson.'

'Well,' said Mr Wilson, 'I have a shop in Coburg Square. Business is not very good. A young man works for me, but I don't pay him much.'

'What is the name of this kind young man?' asked Sherlock Holmes.

'His name is Vincent Spaulding. He's a good man. I am surprised that he stays with me.'

'I am surprised too,' said Holmes. 'There aren't many people like Vincent Spaulding.'

'There is one problem with him,' said Mr Wilson. 'He is a hard-working man, but he likes taking photographs. He spends a lot of time in an underground room below the shop, where he works on his photographs. Well, one day he came to me and showed me this newspaper. He was sorry, he said, that he did not have red hair. "Why?" I asked. "Because there is a free place in the Red-Headed League and the League pays its men very well." I did not know what the Red-Headed League was, Mr Holmes, so I asked him.

' "You do not know of the League?" said Spaulding. "I am surprised. You can join if you want to."

' "How much does the League pay its men?"

' "Four pounds a week. The work is very easy and the hours of work are short. You can work in your shop too."

' "Tell me more," I said.

' "The League has a free place. It says so here in the newspaper. You can go to this address and ask about it. The newspaper says that an American, Ezekiah Hopkins, started the League. He was very rich. He had bright red hair and left all his money to the League. Now the League gives the money to red-headed men."

' "But there are millions of red-headed men!"

' "They can't all join the League. You have to be over twenty-one years old and live in London. Ezekiah Hopkins lived in London for a few years and he loved the city. Also your hair has to be bright red. Not light red. Not dark red. It has to be the colour of fire. You should go, Mr Wilson. The League will give you the place. Think of it! Four pounds a week."

'You can see my hair, Mr Holmes. It is bright red. I decided to go to the address, and Vincent Spaulding offered to come with me. We closed the shop and went to Fleet Street.

'There was a crowd of men in Fleet Street, all of them with red hair. We found the building and Spaulding took my arm. He pulled me through the crowd, into the building and up some stairs. We went into an office.

'There was a table and two chairs in the office. A small man was sitting behind the table. He had bright red hair like mine. The other men who were waiting in the office also all had red hair. The man behind the table spoke to each of them but found something wrong with each one. Then it was my turn. The small man stood up, went to the door and closed it.

'Vincent Spaulding said, "This is Mr Jabez Wilson. He would like to join the League."

'The small man looked at me. "Very good," he said. "Your hair is bright red. A better red than any of the other men. Is it real? I shall check." He came to me and pulled my hair. "Yes, it is real. The place in the League is yours. You can join the Red-Headed League." Then he went to the window. "You can all go home," he shouted. "The free place is now filled." All the red-headed men started to leave and soon the street was empty.

' "My name," he said, "is Duncan Ross. I work for the Red-Headed League. Now, Mr Wilson, when can you start work?"

' "There is a problem," I said. "I have a shop."

' "I will look after the shop," Vincent Spaulding offered.

' "What are the hours of work?" I asked.

' "From ten o'clock until two o'clock, six days a week."

' "Good," I said. "Mr Spaulding can look after the shop in the morning and I shall be there in the afternoon. How much will you pay me?"

' "Four pounds a week."

' "What is the work?"

17

' "It is very easy. You come here at ten o'clock and leave at two o'clock. But you have to stay in the office all the time and not leave it for any reason. If you do, you will lose your place."

' "It's only four hours a day," I said. "I won't leave the office."

' "And you have to come every day except Sunday. You must not miss a day," said Mr Duncan Ross.

' "And the work?"

' "Copying a dictionary. Bring your own pens and paper. You will work at this table. Can you start work tomorrow?"

' "Yes, I'll be here at ten o'clock."

'The next day I left Vincent Spaulding in the shop. I bought some paper and pens and then went to Fleet Street. I arrived at the office at ten o'clock. Mr Duncan Ross was waiting for me. There was a dictionary on the table. I started to copy the dictionary. Mr Ross then left. During the morning he came to see me four times. I left the office at two o'clock.

'This continued for the rest of the week. On Saturday Mr Ross gave me four pounds. It was the same for the next month. Every Saturday Mr Ross gave me four pounds. At first he came to see me every day but after a month he only came on Saturdays. The work was easy and the League paid me well, so I was quite happy.

'This continued for eight weeks. I started at A and reached R in the dictionary. Then suddenly my work came to an end.'

'Came to an end?' said Holmes. 'When?'

'This morning. I went to the office as usual at ten o'clock. The door was shut and there was a note on it. Here it is. You can read it yourself.'

Mr Wilson gave Holmes a card. On it was written: 'The Red-Headed League has closed, 9 October 1890.'

Sherlock Holmes and I looked at the card. We looked at Mr Wilson's sad face and both started to laugh. Mr Wilson was angry.

'A small man was sitting behind the table. He had bright red hair like mine.'

'Why are you laughing?' he asked. 'If you are laughing at me, I shall leave.' He stood up.

'Please sit down, Mr Wilson,' said Holmes. 'We are sorry that we laughed. But it's a very strange story. Please continue. What did you do then?'

Mr Wilson sat down again. 'The note was a great surprise to me, so I visited the other offices in the building. Nobody knew anything about the League. I found the man who owned the building. He did not know about the League or about Mr Duncan Ross.

' "Well," I said, "he's the man who was in room number four."

' "The red-headed man? Oh," he said, "his name is William Morris. He has moved to a new office."

' "Do you know the address?"

' "Yes, it's 17 Edward Street."

'I went to Edward Street, Mr Holmes. Number 17 was a shop. Nobody there knew Mr Duncan Ross.'

'And what did you do then?' asked Holmes.

'I went home,' said Mr Wilson. 'I spoke to Vincent Spaulding. I asked him what I should do. He said that I should wait for a letter from Mr Ross. I knew your name, Mr Holmes. You help people who are in trouble. So I have come to you.'

'You have done the right thing,' said Holmes. 'I shall be happy to help you. This is a strange business and I think it's important. We shall see. But I need more facts. Tell me, Mr Wilson, when did Vincent Spaulding start working for you?'

'Three months ago.'

'When did he first speak about the League?'

'After about a month.'

'How did you find him?'

'I put a card in my window.'

'Was he the only person who came for the job?'

'No. A lot of men wanted it.'

20

'Why did you choose Vincent Spaulding?'

'He offered to work for half the usual pay.'

'I see. Is he very young?'

'No. He's thirty. He is small and quite fat and has a white mark above his right eye.'

Holmes sat up in surprise. 'Has he really?' he cried.

'Do you know him, Holmes?' I asked.

'I think so,' said Holmes. 'When you were working for the League, did Vincent Spaulding do his work well?'

'Yes,' said Mr Wilson. 'The shop is not very busy in the morning. There isn't much work.'

'And he was always alone in the shop?'

'Yes.'

'Thank you, Mr Wilson. That is all that I need to know. Come back next week. Today is Saturday. By Monday I shall know the complete story.'

Mr Wilson left.

'Well, Watson,' said Holmes, 'what do you think of his story?'

'It's a mystery to me,' I replied.

'Yes, it is a mystery, but we shall soon know the answer to it.'

'What are you going to do?' I asked.

'I am going to think, Watson. Please don't speak to me for fifty minutes.'

Holmes closed his eyes. He did not move for three-quarters of an hour. I was beginning to think that he was asleep. Suddenly he jumped out of his chair.

'There is a concert this afternoon,' he said. 'Are you free, Watson?'

'I have nothing to do today.'

'Then come with me. You will enjoy the music. On the way, I want to stop at Coburg Square. We can look at Mr Wilson's shop. Then we'll go to the concert. Come on, Watson.'

We took a carriage to Coburg Square. The buildings in the

'Could you tell me the way to the Strand?'

square were small and old.

'So this,' said Holmes, 'is Mr Wilson's place.'

We were standing in front of a shop. Mr Wilson's name was written above the door. Holmes looked at the building. He walked down the street and then he returned to the shop. He hit the ground with his stick three times. Then he went to the door and pulled the bell. A young man appeared.

'What do you want?' he asked.

'Could you tell me the way to the Strand?'

'First right, second left,' said the young man and he closed the door.

Holmes came to me.

'Do you know that man?' I asked.

'Yes, I do,' said Holmes.

'Did you talk to him because you wanted to see his face?'

'I did not want to see his face.'

'What did you want to see?'

'The knees of his trousers.'

'What did they tell you?'

'Just what I wanted to know, Watson. I'll explain later.'

'Why did you hit the ground in front of the shop?'

'My dear Doctor, we haven't time to talk. We can't stay here. We have seen Coburg Square. Now I want to see behind it.'

Behind Coburg Square there was a wide road which was quite different from Coburg Square. The buildings were tall and new. There were a lot of shops and one large bank, the City Bank.

'Very good,' said Holmes. 'We have finished our work, Doctor. Now it's time to play. We can go to the concert. Ah, music! I shall forget the Red-Headed League for an hour or two.'

◆

Two hours later, we came out of the concert.

'Are you going home now, Doctor?' asked Holmes.

'Yes,' I replied. 'My wife is waiting for me.'

'I have to do something,' said Holmes. 'It will take a few hours. This business in Coburg Square is very important.'

'Why?'

'There is going to be a crime.'

'A crime? Can we stop it?'

'Yes,' said Holmes. 'But it will be difficult. Today is Saturday. The crime will take place tonight. I shall need your help.'

'What time shall I come?'

'Ten o'clock will be early enough.'

'I shall be at Baker Street at ten.'

'Thank you, Doctor. And it will be dangerous, so bring your gun.'

Later that evening I went to Baker Street. Two carriages were standing at the door. When I went in, Holmes was talking to two men. I knew one of them, Inspector Lestrade of Scotland Yard. I did not know the other man.

'Ha! Now we are all here,' said Holmes. He put on his coat and hat and picked up a very heavy stick. 'Watson, you know my friend Inspector Lestrade. And this is Mr Merryweather. He is coming on our adventure.'

'We are working together again, Doctor,' said Lestrade. 'Holmes discovers the crime and then sends for me. Together we catch the thieves.'

'If there are any thieves,' said Mr Merryweather.

'Mr Holmes is usually right,' said Inspector Lestrade.

'Very well,' said Mr Merryweather. 'But I am missing my game of cards. I always play cards on a Saturday night.'

'This game will be more exciting,' said Holmes. 'The winner gets thirty thousand pounds.'

'And if I win, I will get John Clay,' added Lestrade. 'I would very much like to see him in prison.'

'You will catch him tonight,' said Holmes. 'It's ten o'clock.

Let's go now. You two take the first carriage. Watson and I will follow in the second.'

We started for Coburg Square. When we were nearly there, Holmes said, 'Merryweather works for the City Bank. That is the bank near Coburg Square. And that is where we will see the crime.'

We reached Coburg Square. Inspector Lestrade and Mr Merryweather were waiting for us. We looked at Mr Wilson's shop. All was quiet. Then we went to the City Bank. Mr Merryweather opened the door and we went in. We went through a heavy door and down some steps into an underground room. There were piles of big boxes down there.

'Nobody can get in from above,' said Holmes.

'And it's impossible from below,' said Mr Merryweather. He hit the ground with his stick. 'Oh! What a strange noise! Do you think there's a hole under this floor?'

'Please be quiet!' said Holmes. 'They will hear you. Sit on one of those boxes and don't do anything.'

'I'm sorry,' said Mr Merryweather. He sat on a box. Holmes studied the floor closely and then stood up again.

'We have at least an hour to wait,' he said. 'They will start after Mr Wilson goes to bed in the rooms above his shop. Then they will act. They will work quickly because they want to get away fast. Well, Doctor, we are below the City Bank. You can see all these boxes. Mr Merryweather will explain what is in them.'

'Gold,' said Mr Merryweather quietly. 'Thirty thousand gold pieces. We bought them six months ago.'

'And now,' said Holmes, 'let's get ready. Cover the light or they'll see us.'

'And sit in the dark?' said Mr Merryweather.

'I'm afraid so. Our enemy is near. Now let's choose our places. These men are dangerous. I shall stand behind this box. The rest of you can hide behind those boxes. When I shine the light on

John Clay and his friend, jump on them. Watson, it is possible that they have guns. You have yours. Don't be afraid to use it.'

I put my gun on the box in front of me. Holmes covered the light and the room was completely dark.

'They can only get away through the shop in Coburg Square,' said Holmes quietly. 'Is someone waiting there, Lestrade?'

'Four policemen,' Lestrade answered.

'Then they can't get away. And now we should be quiet.'

We waited and the minutes passed slowly. I was cold but I was afraid to move. There was complete silence. Then, after an hour and a quarter, I suddenly saw a very small spot of light in the floor. It changed to a line of light and slowly got wider. The floor was opening. A white hand appeared and then it went back into the ground. The light went off. A few minutes later we heard a loud noise and saw a bigger hole in the floor. Light shone out of it. A head appeared and a man climbed through the hole. A second man, who had bright red hair, followed him.

Sherlock Holmes shone our light on them. Then he jumped from behind the box and caught the first man. The light shone on a gun, but Holmes's heavy stick came down on the man's hand and the gun fell to the floor. The red-headed man jumped back into the hole.

'Don't move, John Clay,' said Holmes. 'Dr Watson's gun is on you. You can't get away now.'

'So I see,' he answered. 'But my friend has.'

'Four policemen are waiting for him in Coburg Square,' said Holmes.

'Oh, really. You have done well.'

'And so have you,' said Holmes. 'Your Red-Headed League was a very good idea. It almost worked.'

Lestrade picked up John Clay's gun. 'And now come with me,' he said. They left the room and we followed them.

'Mr Holmes,' said Merryweather, 'how can I thank you? You

The light shone on a gun, but Holmes's heavy stick came down on the man's hand and the gun fell to the floor.

have saved the bank's gold and caught two dangerous men.'

'I enjoyed it very much,' said Holmes, 'and the bank will pay me for my trouble. I wanted to catch John Clay and it was an adventure. I also enjoyed the story of the Red-Headed League.'

◆

We arrived at Baker Street at four in the morning. Holmes made some coffee.

'It really was a good idea,' said Holmes.

'The Red-Headed League? When did you know what they were doing?'

'When I heard Mr Wilson's story,' answered Holmes. 'There was the piece in the newspaper about the League and then Mr Wilson had to copy a dictionary. In Fleet Street. Why?'

'Someone wanted Mr Wilson to leave the shop,' I said.

'That's right, Watson.'

'But why the Red-Headed League?' I asked.

'John Clay's friend had red hair. That gave Clay the idea. They put the piece in the newspaper and offered four pounds a week. It wasn't much to them because they were going to get thirty thousand pounds. One man has an office and the other man takes Mr Wilson there. What is the result? Mr Wilson leaves Spaulding alone in the shop. Spaulding worked for half the usual pay. He had a reason. The shop was a small one and there was nothing to steal in it. So what did Spaulding want? It wasn't in the shop but it had to be near it. Spaulding took photographs and spent a lot of time in the room below the shop. Underground! The answer lay down there. When we went to the shop, I saw Spaulding and remembered him. His real name is John Clay and the list of his crimes is a long one. He was doing something underground which took a long time. What was it? He was digging. That had to be the answer. He was digging towards another building. You

28

remember our first visit to Coburg Square, Watson? What did I do first?'

'You hit the ground with your stick.'

'I was looking for the hole that he was making,' said Holmes. 'It was not in front of the shop. Then I went to the shop and saw John Clay. There was earth on the knees of his trousers. He stopped digging to open the door. So which building was he digging towards? I went into the street behind Coburg Square and saw the City Bank at the back of Mr Wilson's shop. That was the answer to the problem.'

'You knew when to go to the bank. How?'

'They closed the League's office. That was a sign that the digging was finished. They had to act quickly before Mr Wilson discovered their work. Saturday night was the best time because it gave them almost two days to get away. Poor Clay!'

'Why do you say that, Holmes?'

'He did all that work for nothing.'

The Boscombe Lake Mystery

My wife and I were having breakfast one morning when a note arrived from Sherlock Holmes. It said: 'Are you free for two days? I have just received a message from the West of England. I am going to work on the Boscombe Lake mystery. Will you come with me? The train leaves Paddington Station at 11.15.'

'Are you going, dear?' asked my wife.

'I don't know. I'm quite busy at the moment.'

'Oh, Dr Anstruther will do your work. You look tired and a change will be good for you.'

'Very well. I'll go. But I shall have to pack now. The train leaves in half an hour.'

Twenty-five minutes later, I arrived at Paddington Station. Holmes was waiting for me.

'I'm happy that you could come, Watson,' he said. 'I shall need your help.'

We got into the train. Holmes was carrying some newspapers. He began to read them and to make notes. Suddenly he asked, 'Have you read about Boscombe Lake, Watson?'

'No. I was just going to read about it when your note arrived.'

'The London newspapers are full of it. I have just read them all. The problem seems easy to solve, but it is probably very difficult.'

'Please explain, Holmes,' I said. 'How can it be easy and difficult at the same time?'

'The police think that there is no mystery. A man is dead. They say that his son killed him.'

'Did his son kill him?'

'I don't know. We are going to Boscombe Lake to find out. It's a country area. There are a few villages and some farms. The largest farm belongs to a man called John Turner. He is quite rich. He made his money in Australia and a few years ago he returned to England.

'Mr Turner had a friend from Australia called Charles McCarthy. Mr McCarthy lived on one of Mr Turner's farms. He had less money than Turner, but the two men seemed to be good friends. They were often seen together.

'McCarthy had a son of eighteen and Turner had a daughter of the same age, but both their wives were dead. The families lived very quietly. Turner, of course, was much richer and lived in a large house. Four women and two men worked there. McCarthy's house was quite small and there was just one girl working for him. That is all I know about the families. Now I'll tell you about the story.

'Last Monday Mr McCarthy went to the village and came back at two o'clock. He spoke to the girl who worked for him. He asked her to make him a meal. He told her to hurry because he had to meet someone at Boscombe Lake at three o'clock. He said that it was very important. He left the house just before three o'clock and never returned.

'Boscombe Lake is ten minutes' walk from Mr McCarthy's house. Two people saw him while he was walking towards the lake. One was an old woman. The other was a Mr William Crowder. He works for Mr Turner, Mr McCarthy's friend. Both the old woman and Mr Crowder say that Mr McCarthy was alone.

'Mr Crowder also saw Mr McCarthy's son. The boy was following his father and had a gun under his arm. That evening Mr Crowder heard that Mr McCarthy was dead.

'A girl called Patience Moran also saw Mr McCarthy and his son. She is fourteen and lives near the lake. Patience Moran was picking flowers in the woods. When she reached the lake, she saw Mr McCarthy and his son. They seemed to be fighting. Mr

31

McCarthy was shouting at his son and his son's hand was in the air. Patience thought that he was going to hit his father. She was frightened, so she ran home. She told her mother and father about the fight.

'Soon after that, young McCarthy arrived at the girl's house. He said that his father was dead. He found him when he was out for a walk. The boy didn't have his gun or his hat with him and there was blood on his shirt.

'Mr Moran, the girl's father, went with young McCarthy to the lake. The body of Mr McCarthy was lying on the grass. There was blood coming from his head. Young McCarthy's gun and hat were near the body. Later the police went to McCarthy's house and he was taken to the police station. The police think that he killed his father.'

'Do you think so, Holmes?' I asked.

'I am not sure, but it is possible. It seems from the facts that the killer was young McCarthy. But one person does not think so. That person is Mr Turner's daughter. She has asked me to help young McCarthy.'

'That will be difficult, Holmes, if all the facts are against him. What did young McCarthy say to the police?' I asked.

'The police arrived at the lake two hours after Mr McCarthy died. His son was at home so the police went to his house. They asked him to go with them to the police station. He said that he was not surprised.'

'Because he killed his father?'

'No,' said Holmes. 'He then said that he did not kill his father.'

'Was he lying?'

'No, I think it was true. He knew that the facts were all against him. So when the police came for him he was not surprised.'

'What is the young man's story?'

'It's here in this newspaper,' said Holmes.

I took the newspaper. The report said:

Mr James McCarthy, the son of the dead man, said: 'After three days in Bristol, I returned home last Monday afternoon. My father was not at home. The girl who works for us was alone there. I asked her where my father was. She told me that he was out. I decided to go for a walk and I took my gun with me. I always take my gun because shooting is my favourite sport.

'While I was walking towards Boscombe Lake, I passed William Crowder's house. He saw me. He told the police that I was following my father. That was not true. I did not know that my father was also walking towards the lake.

'I was not far from the lake when I heard a cry of "Cooee!" My father often called me in this way, so I hurried to the lake. My father was there but he was surprised to see me. He asked me why I was there.

'We talked and then my father became very angry. So I left him and started to walk home. After a few minutes I heard a terrible cry. I ran back to the lake. My father was lying on the ground. It was clear that he was badly hurt. I dropped my gun and held him in my arms but he died. Then I went to Mr Moran's house. I asked him to help me. I saw nobody near my father. I don't know who killed him.'

Inspector Lestrade of Scotland Yard then questioned McCarthy.

Lestrade:	Did your father say anything before he died?
McCarthy:	He said a few words, but they were not clear. I only heard the word "rat".
Lestrade:	Why did he say that?
McCarthy:	I don't know.
Lestrade:	Why were you fighting with your father?
McCarthy:	I can't answer that question.
Lestrade:	You refuse to answer? That won't help you.
McCarthy:	I refuse.
Lestrade:	Now, was the cry of "Cooee!" the usual sign between you and your father?

McCarthy:	It was.
Lestrade:	But he thought that you were in Bristol. Why did he call to you?
McCarthy:	I don't know.
Lestrade:	You found your father near the lake, lying on the ground. Did you see anything strange in the area?
McCarthy:	I think I saw something. It was grey. Perhaps it was a coat. When I was leaving to get help, I looked for it. I could not find it.
Lestrade:	How far was it from the body?
McCarthy:	About 30 feet.
Lestrade:	And from the beginning of the woods?
McCarthy:	About the same.
Lestrade:	You did not see the person who took it?
McCarthy:	No. It was behind me.

That was young McCarthy's story.

We arrived in the town of Ross, near Boscombe Lake. Inspector Lestrade was waiting for us there. We were driven in a carriage to the Ross Hotel, where we were staying. We went to our rooms and asked for some tea.

'I have ordered a carriage for you,' said Lestrade. 'You can drive to Boscombe Lake before dark.'

'Thank you, Lestrade,' said Holmes. 'But I am not going out tonight.'

Lestrade laughed. 'So you are quite clear about the facts. Young McCarthy killed his father. I don't understand Miss Turner's request to you. There is nothing that you can do. You will have to tell her that. And here she is. Her carriage has just stopped at the door.'

The door opened and a beautiful woman came in. Her eyes were shining. She was very excited.

'Oh, Mr Sherlock Holmes!' she cried. 'I am so happy that you could come. James McCarthy did not kill his father. I knew James when we were children. I know him better than anyone. He is not perfect, but he is a good, kind person.'

'I shall try to help him,' said Holmes.

'You have heard the story, Mr Holmes. Do you think that James killed his father?'

'No, I don't think that he killed him,' said Holmes.

'There now!' cried Miss Turner. 'You heard Mr Holmes, Inspector Lestrade.'

'I don't agree with Mr Holmes,' said Lestrade.

'But he is right,' said Miss Turner. 'James did not do it. He did not explain the fight with his father. But I know what they fought about. Mr McCarthy wanted James to marry me. But James loved me in the way that a brother loves a sister. He did not want to marry me. James and his father often fought about it.'

'Did your father want you to marry James?' asked Holmes.

'No, he was against the idea,' Miss Turner replied.

'Thank you, Miss Turner. This is very important. I would like to see your father. Can I come to your house tomorrow?'

'I'm afraid that he is very ill. The doctor says he can't have visitors.'

'When did your father become ill?' asked Holmes.

'A long time ago. But this trouble has made him much worse.'

'I see,' said Holmes. 'Tell me, Miss Turner, where did your father meet Mr McCarthy?'

'In Australia, at the mines.'

'Yes, at the gold mines. Your father made his money there. Thank you, Miss Turner, you have been very helpful.'

'I need to go to Father now,' said Miss Turner. 'He misses me if I leave him for too long. Goodbye, Mr Holmes.' She hurried from the room.

'That was terrible, Holmes,' said Lestrade. 'Now she thinks that you can help James McCarthy.'

'But I *can* help him,' said Holmes. 'He will soon be free. Can I see him?'

'Of course. I'll take you to him,' said Lestrade.

'Then, Watson, I shall go out tonight after all. I shall be away for two hours.'

It was midnight when Holmes returned. 'I hope it doesn't rain tomorrow,' he said. 'I want to search the ground near Boscombe Lake. I saw young McCarthy.'

'And what did he tell you?'

'He does not know anything about the attack. But he told me the real reason for the fight with his father. Young McCarthy is in love with Miss Turner. But she was away at school for five years and during that time James met a girl in Bristol. He was very young and he married the girl secretly.

'His father told him many times to marry Miss Turner. James wanted to marry her, but it was impossible; he was already married. That's the reason for the fight. James did throw his arms in the air, but he wasn't going to hit his father.'

'Why didn't he tell his father that he was married?' I asked.

'His father was a hard man. James had no money. He had to stay with his father, so he could not tell him. You remember that James went to Bristol for three days? He spent them with his wife.'

'Does his wife know that James is in trouble?' I asked.

'Yes. She has written to him. She says that they were never married. She already had a husband before she met James.'

'James was never really married to her?'

'That's right,' said Holmes. 'That is the only good news that James has had.'

'If James did not kill his father, who did kill him?' I asked.

'Ah! Who? The dead man went to meet someone. It wasn't his son. But it was someone he knew. And he called "Cooee!" to that person.'

◆

The next morning the weather was fine. Lestrade, Holmes and I drove to the McCarthys' house.

'I saw Mr Turner's doctor this morning,' said Lestrade. 'Mr Turner is worse. He's dying. This trouble has made his illness much worse. After all, McCarthy was his friend. He gave McCarthy a house and helped him in many ways.'

'But he did not want his daughter to marry McCarthy's son,' said Holmes. 'That seems rather strange.'

We arrived at the McCarthys' house and a girl opened the door. Holmes asked her for a pair of Mr McCarthy's shoes and a pair of his son's shoes. He measured them. Then we followed the path to Boscombe Lake.

Boscombe Lake was 160 feet wide and lay between Mr Turner's farm and Mr McCarthy's house. On the side near McCarthy's house the woods were thick. From the beginning of the lake to the woods was 65 feet. The ground was very soft and covered with grass.

'Where was the body?' asked Holmes.

Lestrade showed us the place. The mark of the body showed on the soft ground. Holmes searched the area around it.

'Ah!' he said. 'Here are three pairs of marks. These are young McCarthy's footsteps. Twice he was walking, and once he ran quickly. That agrees with his story. He ran to his father when he was on the ground. Here are his father's feet and here is a mark made by a gun. The son was standing here, listening to his father. And what is this? Ha! Someone was walking quietly . . . on his toes! His shoes had square toes. They come. They go. They come again – that was to collect the coat. Where did they come from?' Holmes followed the footsteps to the beginning of the woods and went behind a large tree. He picked up a large stone and put it in his pocket. We then followed a path through the woods and

'Someone was walking quietly . . . on his toes! His shoes had
square toes.'

came to a road. Holmes stopped in front of a house.

'This should be where Mr Moran lives,' said Holmes. 'I want to see him, and perhaps write a little note. You two can wait in the carriage. I'll join you in a few minutes.'

Ten minutes later, we were driving back to our hotel. Holmes took the stone from his pocket.

'Did you see this in the woods, Lestrade?' he asked. 'This stone killed Mr McCarthy.'

'I see no marks or blood on it,' said Lestrade. 'How do you know that it killed McCarthy?'

'The grass was growing under it, so the stone was only put there a few days ago. And the shape of the stone will fit the mark on McCarthy's head.'

'Who killed him then?'

'A tall man,' said Holmes. 'He uses his left hand. He has a bad right leg and wears heavy shoes with square toes. He has a grey coat. You have his description now, Lestrade. You will be able to find him. I shall be busy this afternoon and I shall go back to London tonight.'

'But that description fits a lot of people,' said Lestrade. 'Can't you tell me who it is?'

'Perhaps,' said Holmes. 'I'll send you a note later today.'

Holmes and I went back to the hotel and Lestrade went to the police station.

'Now, Watson,' said Holmes. 'I want to talk about two things in young McCarthy's story. His father's cry of "Cooee!" and the word "rat".'

'What about his cry of "Cooee!" then?' I asked.

'He wasn't shouting to his son. He did not know that his son was coming back from Bristol. Australians shout "Cooee!" I think he was shouting to an Australian.'

'What about the word "rat", then?'

Sherlock Holmes took a piece of paper from his pocket. It was a map of Australia. He put his finger over part of the map. 'What does that say?' he asked.

'RAT,' I said.

'And now?' Holmes lifted his finger.

'BALLARAT.'

'That's right, Watson. That was McCarthy's last word. He was naming the person who killed him.'

'Someone from Ballarat!' I said.

'Yes,' agreed Holmes. 'So it was someone who Mr McCarthy knew in Ballarat. He wears a grey coat and his shoes have square toes. He takes long steps, so he has to be tall.'

'You said that he had a bad leg.'

'Yes,' said Holmes. 'His left foot made a deeper mark. He puts less weight on his right foot, so he has a bad right leg.'

'He uses his left hand. How do you know that?'

'He stood behind McCarthy,' said Holmes, 'and hit McCarthy on the left side of his head. So he uses his left hand.'

'Holmes,' I said, 'you have saved young McCarthy. The man who killed his father was –'

At that moment our door opened and the waiter brought in a man. 'Mr John Turner,' he said.

Our visitor was a tall man. He walked slowly because he had a bad right leg. His face was white and he looked very ill.

'Please sit down,' said Holmes quietly. 'You received my note?'

'Yes. Moran brought it to me. Why do you want to see me?'

'Because you killed Mr McCarthy,' said Holmes.

The sick man put his hands over his face. 'You're right,' he cried. 'I was not going to let young McCarthy die for my crime. I was going to go to the police.'

'I'm happy to hear it,' said Holmes.

'I was thinking about my daughter,' said Mr Turner. 'This will break her heart.'

'Perhaps she will not hear about it,' Holmes suggested.

'What?'

'I am not a policeman,' said Holmes. 'Your daughter asked me to come here and I am helping her. I want to save young McCarthy, that is all.'

'I am dying,' said Mr Turner. 'I have about a month to live and I want to die at home.'

Holmes stood up and went to the table. He took a piece of paper and a pen. 'Tell me all about it,' he said. 'I shall write it down, then you will sign it. If the police free young McCarthy, it will stay a secret. If they don't free him, I shall give the paper to them.'

'Thank you,' said Mr Turner. 'I'll tell you everything. It was like this. In 1860 I went to Australia to look for gold but I didn't find any. I was young and I made some bad friends. There were six of us. We stopped people on the roads from the mines and stole their gold.

'One day a lot of gold was travelling from Ballarat to Melbourne. We waited for it. There were six policemen and a driver with the gold. All six policemen were killed and three of my friends also died. I was going to shoot the driver, but I decided not to. The driver's name was McCarthy. I was rich after that. I came back to England and bought my farm. I lived quietly and I tried to forget the past. I married, but my wife died young. She left me with my daughter, Alice. Then McCarthy found us.

'I was walking down Regent Street when I met him. He was dirty and looked very poor. "Here we are, John," he said. "We have come to find you. I have a son and you will look after us both now. If you don't, I shall go to the police."

'They came to the Boscombe area and McCarthy refused to leave. I had to give him a house and some of my best land. I had no rest. I could not forget the past because McCarthy was always

41

there. Alice grew up and I became more and more frightened. I did not want her to learn about my past. McCarthy knew this and I had to give him money and land. Then he asked for Alice.

'I was ill and McCarthy wanted his son to marry Alice. As a result of the marriage, my land was all going to belong to his family after my death. But I refused. I had nothing against the boy, but I hated his father. I could not give my daughter to his son. McCarthy said that he was going to go to the police. He sent me a note saying that it was my last chance. He told me to meet him at the lake.

'When I went to the lake, McCarthy was talking to his son. He was ordering him to marry my daughter. This made me very angry, so I waited behind a tree. I decided then to kill McCarthy. When his son left, I picked up a large stone. He had his back to me. So I walked up to him and hit him hard. He gave a terrible cry and this brought back his son. I hid in the woods, but my coat was still next to the lake. Very quietly I went back and got it. Young McCarthy did not see me. That is the true story, Mr Holmes.'

Holmes wrote the last word and Mr Turner signed the paper.

'I shall keep this,' said Holmes. 'It is possible that the police will free young McCarthy without it. If they do, I shall keep your secret.'

'Goodbye, then,' said Mr Turner, 'and thank you, Mr Holmes. You have made my last days happy.' He walked slowly from the room.

Holmes went to the police and told them about his discoveries near the lake. They freed James McCarthy. Mr Turner only lived for another six months. A year later, James McCarthy married Alice Turner. They never knew the true story.

The Blue Diamond

One day last winter I went to see Sherlock Holmes. I remember the date; it was 27 December. Holmes was sitting in a comfortable chair, looking at an old hat.

'Are you busy, Holmes?' I asked.

'Not at all, Watson,' he answered. 'I'm happy to see you. You know our friend Peterson, the hotel doorman. He brought me this hat and a chicken. Peterson is going to eat the chicken today. Sit down. I'll tell you the story.

'Two days ago, after a party, Peterson was walking along Goodge Street. It was three o'clock in the morning. By the light of the street lights he saw a tall man in front of him, carrying a chicken under his arm. Suddenly two other men came out of the shadows and stopped the tall man. A fight started. One of the attackers hit the tall man and his hat fell to the ground. The tall man tried to hit his attacker with his stick but missed him. His stick broke a shop window. Peterson ran to help the tall man. He saw Peterson's clothes and ran away down the street. In the dark, of course, Peterson looks like a policeman. The tall man's attackers followed him. A hat and a chicken were left on the ground.'

'Why didn't Peterson give them back to the tall man?' I asked.

'Because the tall man was not there, Watson. But there was a card on the chicken's leg which said, 'For Mrs Henry Baker'. The name Henry Baker is also inside the hat. Peterson wanted to find the man, but there are hundreds of Henry Bakers in London.'

'So what did he do?'

'He brought the hat and the chicken to me,' said Holmes. 'He knows that these little problems interest me. I kept the chicken until today, but I couldn't keep it any longer. Peterson is

43

probably eating it now.'

At that moment the door opened and Peterson ran into the room. He was very excited.

'The chicken, Mr Holmes! The chicken!' he cried.

'What's the matter?' asked Holmes. 'Has it come back to life and flown through the window?'

'Look at this!' cried Peterson. 'My wife found it inside the chicken.' He held out his hand. In it was a beautifully cut blue stone which shone in the light.

'Well, well!' cried Holmes. 'Do you know what this is, Peterson?'

'It's a diamond,' said Peterson, 'a very expensive diamond.'

'It is more than just a diamond,' said Holmes. 'It's the famous blue diamond.'

'Not Lady Morcar's blue diamond?' I asked.

'Of course it is,' said Holmes. 'I know its size and shape because I read about it in the newspapers. Lady Morcar is offering a thousand pounds to get it back.'

'A thousand pounds!' said Peterson. 'Then it is a twenty-thousand-pound stone.'

'It was stolen from Lady Morcar at the Cosmopolitan Hotel,' I remembered.

'That's right,' said Holmes. 'It was stolen on 22 December, just five days ago. The police say that a man called John Horner stole it. There was a report in the newspaper.' Holmes searched through a pile of newspapers. 'Ah, here it is:

'Lady Morcar's diamond stolen. Lady Morcar was staying at the Cosmopolitan Hotel when, on 22 December, the famous blue diamond was stolen from her room. The police think that the thief is a man called John Horner. Horner is twenty-six and works at the hotel. James Ryder, a waiter at the hotel, saw a broken table in Lady Morcar's room earlier in the day. He asked Horner to repair it. He went with Horner

44

At that moment the door opened and Peterson ran into the room.

to the room and showed him the table. Ryder had to leave the room for a few minutes; when he returned, the room was empty. A broken box was lying on the floor. The police say that Lady Morcar kept the blue diamond in that box. They questioned Horner. He said that he did not see either the box or the diamond. Horner is known to the police because he once stole some money from a hotel room.

'That is the story,' said Holmes. 'Only we know the ending.'

'Yes,' said Peterson. 'It ended with the diamond inside a chicken.'

'The diamond disappeared from Lady Morcar's room,' I said. 'How did it get inside a chicken?'

'You see, Watson,' said Holmes. 'The old hat and the chicken are important now. Now we have a crime. Here is the blue diamond which was found in a chicken. Mr Henry Baker had the chicken, so the next step is to find Mr Baker. We will do that through the newspaper. Give me a pencil and a piece of paper, Watson. Now then: "Found in Goodge Street – a chicken and a black hat. Will Mr Henry Baker come to 221B, Baker Street. He will find his hat and his chicken there." I'll put this in the newspaper.'

'Will Henry Baker see it?' I asked.

'I hope so,' said Holmes. 'Peterson, you go past the newspaper office, don't you? Will you give this to them?'

'Of course,' said Peterson. 'But what are you going to do with the diamond?'

'Ah, yes,' said Holmes. 'I shall keep the diamond and return it to Lady Morcar later. Thank you, Peterson.'

Peterson went out.

'Mr Henry Baker will come for his chicken,' said Holmes. 'I'll buy another one for him.' Holmes held the diamond against the light. 'It's a beautiful stone,' he said. 'I'll put it in a safe place. Then I'll send a note to Lady Morcar. She will be very pleased.'

'Did John Horner steal it?' I asked.

'He says that he did not steal it,' said Holmes.

'How did Henry Baker get it, then?'

'Henry Baker did not steal the blue diamond either. The diamond was in his chicken but he did not know that. He knows nothing about the diamond. I shall soon be sure about that.'

'When?'

'When he comes to get his chicken.'

'And you can do nothing until then?'

'Nothing,' said Holmes.

'Very well,' I said. 'I shall go now. I have some work to do. I'll come back this evening. I would like to know the end of the story.'

'I shall be happy to see you,' said Holmes. 'Come and have dinner with me. I'm having chicken.' He laughed. 'I'll look inside it. Perhaps I'll find a diamond.'

That evening I went back to Baker Street. A tall man was standing at Holmes's door. Holmes opened it. 'Mr Henry Baker, I think,' he said. 'Please come in. Ah, Watson, you have come at the right time.'

We all went up to Holmes's room.

'Please sit near the fire,' said Holmes. 'It's a cold night.' Holmes picked up the old hat. 'Is this your hat, Mr Baker?' he asked.

'Yes, it is.'

Henry Baker was a tall man with grey hair. His clothes were old and he looked poor.

'I have kept your hat for you,' said Holmes.

'Thank you,' said Henry Baker. 'I did not think that I was going to see it again. Some men attacked me in the street.'

'But someone has eaten your chicken,' said Holmes.

'Eaten!' cried Henry Baker. 'Why have I come here, then?'

'I have another chicken,' said Holmes. 'You can have that. It's the same size and it's quite fresh too. Would you like it?'

'Of course,' said Henry Baker. 'Thank you very much.'

'Here is the chicken and your hat,' said Holmes. 'Can I ask one question? Where did you buy the other chicken?'

'I bought it from Mr Windigate. He owns the Alpha Hotel, which is near the library in Bloomsbury. I am not working at the moment and I spend most of my days in the library. I am a poor man, so I paid Mr Windigate a few pence each week over the last few months. The chicken was for Christmas. Thank you for my hat, Mr Holmes. I need it. It's a cold night.' Then he left.

Holmes closed the door behind him. 'We can forget about Mr Henry Baker,' he said. 'He knows nothing about the diamond. Are you hungry, Watson?'

'I'm not very hungry.'

'Then we can eat later. We have work to do.'

We walked quickly through the streets of London. It was very cold, the sky was clear and the stars were shining in the night sky. A quarter of an hour later, we arrived at the Alpha Hotel. We went in and Holmes asked for Mr Windigate.

When he came to us, Holmes said, 'I'd like to buy some of your chickens.'

'They are not my chickens,' said Mr Windigate. 'I buy them in Covent Garden market.'

'I see,' said Holmes. 'Who sells them to you?'

'A man called Breckenridge.'

A few minutes later, we were walking towards Covent Garden market.

'We are going to see Mr Breckenridge,' said Holmes. 'He sold the chicken with the diamond in it. Where did he get the chicken? That is the next question.'

We arrived at the market and soon found Mr Breckenridge. He was getting ready to leave.

'Good evening,' said Holmes. 'Have you sold all your chickens?'

'Yes,' said Breckenridge. 'But I shall have some more tomorrow.'

'That's too late.'

'They have some over there.'

'But I was told to come to you.'

'Who told you to come to me?'

'Mr Windigate at the Alpha Hotel.'

'Ah, yes – I sold about twenty to him.'

'They were very good,' said Holmes. 'Where did you buy them?'

'Why do you want to know?' asked Breckenridge. He was angry now.

'It is not important,' said Holmes. 'Why are you angry?'

'Because I'm tired of people like you,' said Breckenridge. 'Another man has been here five or six times. I got tired of his stupid questions. He asked where the chickens were. Then he wanted to know who bought them. I was very busy, so I told him to go away.'

'I don't know the other person,' said Holmes. 'My friend and I had one of the chickens from the Alpha Hotel and it was very good. My friend says it was a town bird. I say that it came from the country.'

'Then you are wrong,' said Breckenridge. 'Those chickens were London birds.'

'That's not possible,' said Holmes.

'What reason is there to lie about it?' shouted Breckenridge. He was angry again. He picked up a book. 'Look here. It's in my book. "December 22. Twenty chickens bought from Mrs Oakshott, 117 Brixton Road. Sold to Mr Windigate at the Alpha Hotel." So, my clever friend, you are wrong.'

'I'm very sorry,' said Holmes. 'Please excuse me.'

We left Mr Breckenridge and walked along the street. Holmes was laughing. 'Well, Watson,' he said, 'that's what I wanted know.

We are near the end of this mystery. We will solve it at Mrs Oakshott's.'

Suddenly we heard a noise behind us. Breckenridge was fighting with a small man.

'I'm tired of you and your chickens,' he shouted. 'I bought them from Mrs Oakshott.'

'But one of them was mine,' said the little man.

'Go and see Mrs Oakshott, then.'

'She told me to see you.'

'Oh, go away!' shouted Breckenridge. He lifted his hand to hit the little man. The little man ran down the street.

'Come on, Watson,' said Holmes. 'Perhaps this will save us a visit to Mrs Oakshott. We have to catch that man.' We ran after him and Holmes took his arm. The little man stopped and turned round. He looked frightened.

'Who are you?' asked the little man. 'What do you want?'

'Excuse me,' said Holmes. 'You were talking to Mr Breckenridge. I heard what you said. I can help you.'

'How can you help me?'

'My name is Sherlock Holmes. You are trying to find some chickens that Mrs Oakshott sold to Mr Breckenridge. He sold them to Mr Windigate of the Alpha Hotel, and then Mr Windigate sold one of them to Mr Henry Baker.'

'Then I would like to talk to you,' said the little man. He was very excited.

A carriage was passing and Holmes stopped it.

'Come with me to my rooms,' said Holmes. 'We can talk there. What is your name?'

The little man did not answer at first. Then he said, 'My name is John Robinson.'

'No, no, your real name,' said Holmes. 'I have to know your real name.'

The man's face went red. 'My real name is James Ryder.'

Suddenly we heard a noise behind us. Breckenridge was fighting with a small man.

'And you work at the Cosmopolitan Hotel,' said Holmes. 'Please get into the carriage.'

We all climbed in. We said nothing during the drive. Half an hour later we were in Baker Street.

We went into Holmes's room. 'Here we are,' he said. 'Ah, the room is warm. You look cold, Mr Ryder. Please sit near the fire. Now, you want to know about the chickens. Are you looking for a black and white chicken?'

'That's right,' cried Ryder. 'Where is it?'

'It came here.'

'Here?'

'Yes. And there was an egg in it, a beautiful blue egg. I have it here.' Holmes held up the blue diamond. It shone like a star. Ryder stood up and looked wide-eyed at the diamond.

'You are finished, Ryder,' said Holmes. 'You stole this diamond.'

Ryder almost fell to the floor.

'Catch him, Watson,' cried Holmes. 'Sit him in that chair.'

I put Ryder in the chair. His face was white with fear.

'I know most of the facts,' said Holmes. 'But I would like to know the complete story. Who told you about the blue diamond?'

'Catherine Cusack told me about it,' he said. 'She works for Lady Morcar.'

'I see,' said Holmes. 'She told you where the diamond was. You were poor but you wanted to be rich. So you stole the blue diamond. You knew that John Horner once stole some money from a hotel room. So you decided to make him the thief. You broke the table in Lady Morcar's room. Repairing things was Horner's job in the hotel. You took him to Lady Morcar's room. He repaired the table and then he left. You knew that the diamond was in the box. You opened it and took the diamond. Then you went to the police and told them about Horner. You then–'

Ryder suddenly fell on his knees. 'Please,' he cried, 'please think of my mother and father. This will break their hearts. I am not a thief. This was the first time. Don't tell the police!'

'Get back into your chair!' said Holmes. 'It is too late now. You stole the blue diamond and called John Horner a thief. That was a terrible thing to do. I have to save John Horner, so I have to tell the police about you.'

'I'll go away. I'll leave the country,' said Ryder. 'Tell the police then.'

'Perhaps,' said Holmes. 'If you tell me the full story.'

'I'll tell you everything,' he said. 'I stole the diamond and told the police about John Horner. They took him to the police station. Then they started to search all the rooms in the hotel, so I left. I went to my sister's house in Brixton Road. She is married to a man called Oakshott. They keep chickens. My sister saw that I was frightened about something. I said that I was tired and thirsty. When she went into the kitchen to make some tea, I went behind the house. They keep the chickens there. I had to hide the diamond. But where? Then I saw the chickens and I had an idea.

'My sister was planning to give me one of the chickens. One of them was black and white. I caught it, opened its mouth and pushed in the diamond. Now the diamond was inside the chicken. Of course it made a lot of noise and my sister came out of the house. When I turned to speak to her, the chicken got away. It ran back to the others. My sister asked me what I was doing.

' "You promised me a chicken," I said. "I'm choosing one."

' "Which one do you want?" she asked.

' "That one," I said. "The black and white one."

' "All right," said my sister. "I'll kill it. You can take it now."

'I know a man in Kilburn who was going to sell the diamond for me. I arrived at his house with the chicken. We opened it, but there was no sign of the diamond. It was the wrong chicken. I went quickly back to my sister's house but none of the chickens were there.

' "Where are the chickens?" I cried.

' "I have sent them to the market," said my sister.

' "Which market?"

' "To Mr Breckenridge at Covent Garden market."

' "Was there another black and white chicken?" I asked.

' "Yes, there were two black and white ones. You took one of them."

'Well, I went to Covent Garden market and saw Mr Breckenridge. He had no chickens. They were all sold. He refused to tell me who bought them. I went back three or four times and his answer was always the same.' Ryder started to cry. 'I am finished,' he said. 'This will kill my mother and father.'

Sherlock Holmes went to the door and opened it. 'Get out!' he said.

'What?' said Ryder. 'Oh, thank you.'

'Don't say any more. Get out!'

Ryder ran out of the room, down the stairs and out of the house.

'After all, Watson,' said Holmes, 'I am not a policeman. Ryder will leave the country. Without him the police will not have a case against Horner, so they will have to free him. I should tell the police. But Ryder is terribly frightened and he has learnt his lesson. I have enjoyed this case. Now, Watson, let us enjoy our dinner. We are having chicken, of course!'

The Single Man

Everyone knows about Lord Simon's marriage and its sudden end. It was four years ago and my friend Sherlock Holmes worked on the problem. The full story was never reported in the newspapers, so here it is.

It was a few weeks before my own wedding and I was living with Holmes in Baker Street. One afternoon a letter arrived for him.

'Good,' said Sherlock Holmes, after he finished reading. 'We have a new job. This letter is from Lord Simon. I'll read it to you.

'My dear Sherlock Holmes,

I have a difficult problem. Lord Backwater suggested that I should see you. He says that you will help me. Can I come to see you? You have probably read about my wedding in the newspapers. Inspector Lestrade is already working on the mystery but I would like you to help. Inspector Lestrade would also be grateful for your help. I will come to Baker Street at four in the afternoon. Please be there. This is very important.

Yours truly,
ROBERT SIMON.'

'He is coming at four o'clock,' I said. 'He will be here in an hour.'

'Then I have just enough time,' said Holmes. 'I can read about the wedding in the newspapers. I also need to read about Lord Simon. You can help me, Watson. Take these papers and cut out all the reports about the wedding.'

Holmes picked up a red book and opened it. 'Here he is,' he

said. 'Robert Walsingham Simon, second son of the Duke of Balmoral. Born in 1846. He's forty-one. That's rather old for a first marriage. The rest is not important. What have you found in the newspapers, Watson?'

'Quite a lot,' I said. 'The story began a few weeks ago. The report says, "Lord Simon plans to marry soon. Lord Simon, the second son of the Duke of Balmoral, is going to marry Miss Hatty Doran. She is the daughter of Mr Aloysius Doran of San Francisco." That is all it says.'

'It's short, but it gives us the facts,' said Holmes.

'There is a longer piece a few days later. Ah, here it is: "Another Englishman from a good family is going to marry an American girl. Lord Simon is forty-one and single. He has now decided to marry and has chosen Miss Hatty Doran. Miss Doran arrived in London six months ago. She is the only daughter of a very rich man from California, Mr Aloysius Doran. Her father's wedding present to her will be a large sum of money. Lord Simon's father is the Duke of Balmoral, who has just had to sell all his pictures. Lord Simon, his son, has little land or money of his own. The marriage will give the lady a title. It will also bring a lot of money into the Simon family." '

'Is there any more?' asked Holmes.

'Oh, yes,' I said, 'there is a lot. The report says that the wedding will be at St George's Church. It will be a quiet wedding because the families only plan to invite a few friends. Lord Simon and his wife will live in Lancaster Gate. Mr Doran is buying a house for them.

'The next report is in yesterday's paper. After the wedding, Miss Doran disappeared.'

'*When* did she disappear?'

'Yesterday. The day of the wedding. Just after it.'

'Did she now? Women often disappear before the wedding. They sometimes disappear a few days later. But the same day!

56

That's very strange.'

'And this report was in today's newspaper.' I read it to him:

'Lady Simon disappears. The family of Lord Robert Simon is very worried today. Yesterday Lord Simon married Miss Hatty Doran, but after the wedding something strange took place. We can now tell our readers the complete story.

'The wedding was at St George's Church. Only a few people were invited. After the wedding, they all went to Mr Aloysius Doran's house in Lancaster Gate. A meal was waiting for them there.

'There was some trouble when a woman tried to get into the house. She said that Lord Simon was going to marry her. He made a promise to her some time ago. She was told to go away and she left.

'Miss Doran was already at the house, but did not see her. Then, during the meal, Miss Doran said that she felt ill. She went up to her room and did not return. Her father went upstairs but could not find her. His daughter was not in the house. A girl who was working there saw Miss Doran leaving.

'Lord Simon and Mr Aloysius Doran went to the police, and the police are now looking for Miss Doran. Some people are saying that she is dead, and the police are holding a woman at the police station.'

'Is that all?' asked Holmes.

'No,' I said 'There is a short report in another newspaper. Here it is: "The police are holding Miss Flora Millar. She became a friend of Lord Simon when she was a dancer at the Allegro Club. She is the woman who tried to get into Mr Aloysius Doran's house at the time of the wedding party."'

'There is the bell, Watson,' said Holmes. 'That will be Lord Simon.'

Lord Simon looked older than forty-one. His hair was grey and he walked like an old man.

'Please sit down, Lord Simon,' said Holmes. 'This is my friend,

Dr Watson. We have read about your wedding in the newspapers. Are the stories true?'

'Yes. But the newspapers don't have all the facts,' said Lord Simon.

'Then I have to ask you some questions,' said Holmes.

'Of course.'

'When and where did you meet Miss Hatty Doran?'

'In San Francisco a year ago. I was travelling in the United States.'

'Did you ask her to marry you then?'

'No. But I liked her very much.'

'Her father is very rich.'

'The richest man in San Francisco.'

'How did he make his money?'

'From a gold mine. He had nothing a few years ago. Then he found gold and now he is very rich.'

'Tell me about your wife.'

'She was twenty when her father found gold. Before that she lived in the gold camps. It was a hard life for a girl and she did not go to school. She led a very free life and educated herself in the fields and the mountains. But she is a good woman and a very honest one.'

'Have you a photograph of her?'

'I brought this one with me.' He gave it to Holmes. Holmes and I looked at it. Hatty Doran was very beautiful.

'So the young lady came to London,' said Holmes. 'And you saw her again.'

'Yes. I fell in love with her and now we are married.'

'She brought you a lot of money.'

'Yes.'

'Will you keep the money?'

'I don't know. The money is not important. I want to find my wife.'

'Of course,' said Holmes. 'Did you see Miss Doran the day before your wedding?'

'Yes.'

'Was she happy?'

'Very happy. She talked about our life together.'

'Was she happy on the morning of the wedding?'

'Yes. But in the church she changed.'

'In what way?'

'It was a small thing. While we were leaving the church, she dropped her flowers. A man picked them up and gave them back to her. On our return to the house she spoke very little.'

'Was this man one of your wife's friends?'

'I don't think so.'

'You returned to the house. What did your wife do then?'

'She spoke to Alice.'

'Who is Alice?'

'She works for my wife. She came from California with her.'

'Are they good friends?'

'Yes. They were always together.'

'What did they say? Could you hear?'

'My wife said something about "jumping a claim". She uses American phrases like that. Sometimes I can't understand her. Then we started our meal. Ten minutes later she felt ill and went out. She never returned.'

'Did anyone see her?'

'Yes. Alice saw her. My wife put on her coat and hat and left the house. Later someone saw her in the park. She was with Flora Millar, the woman who came to the house.'

'Flora Millar is one of your friends.'

'Yes. We were very good friends in the past. She danced at the Allegro. I was good to her and I always gave her a lot of money. She heard that I was going to marry. I know that she was very angry about it. I was afraid of a scandal at the church, so I only

59

invited a few people. Flora came to the house after the wedding. She said that she was going to kill my wife. We kept her out of the house and she left.'

'Did your wife hear all this?'

'No. She knew nothing about it. It was finished in a few moments.'

'Later your wife was in the park with Flora Millar.'

'Yes. Inspector Lestrade says that this is important. It is possible that Flora knows where my wife is.'

'And what do you think?'

'If she does know, Flora will not hurt her.'

'But she was very angry,' said Holmes. 'Perhaps she attacked your wife. Why did your wife run away, Lord Simon? Have you any idea?'

'She was marrying into a very good family and her life was going to change completely. Perhaps she was afraid.'

'That is also possible,' said Holmes. 'There is just one more question. When you were sitting at the table with your wife, what could you see through the window?'

'The road in front of the house, and the park.'

'Thank you,' said Holmes. 'That is all I need. I shall have some news for you soon.'

So Lord Simon left.

A few minutes later Inspector Lestrade arrived, carrying a black bag. He put it down and accepted a cup of tea.

'What is it?' asked Holmes. 'You don't look very happy.'

'I'm not very happy,' said Lestrade. 'I have just spent a day looking for Lady Simon without success.'

'And you are wet,' said Holmes.

'Yes, we were in the park, searching the lake.'

'What were you looking for?'

'Lady Simon's body,' said Lestrade sadly.

Sherlock Holmes laughed. 'You won't find her there,' he said.

'A man picked them up and gave them back to her.'

Lestrade was angry now. 'And you know where she is,' he shouted.

'She is not in the lake,' said Holmes.

'Then how do you explain these?' said Lestrade. He opened the bag that he had with him. From it he took a white dress, a pair of white shoes and some flowers. They were all wet. He put a gold ring on top of the pile. 'What do you think about these? We found them in the lake. They are Lady Simon's clothes, so her body is probably near the lake.'

'I don't think so,' said Holmes. 'My clothes are in the bedroom but I am not always near them. But please continue, Lestrade.'

'I think that Flora Millar killed Lady Simon. I have a note which was in the pocket of the white dress. It says, "When you see me, all will be ready. Come at once. F. H. M." Flora Millar sent this note to Lady Simon. Lady Simon went to the park and Flora Millar killed her.'

Holmes laughed. 'Can I see the note, Lestrade?' he asked. He looked at it. 'This is important.'

'You are reading the wrong side of the note,' said Lestrade. 'The message is on the other side.'

'But this is the side that interests me,' said Holmes. 'It is a hotel bill dated 4 October, for a room and meals. The name of the hotel is not on the bill.'

'That's not important,' said Lestrade. 'Goodbye, Holmes. We shall see who finds Lady Simon first.' He picked up the clothes and put them in the black bag.

'I'll tell you something, Lestrade. There is no Lady Simon and there never was such a person.'

Lestrade laughed. 'I really have to go,' he said. He picked up the bag and hurried out.

Holmes put on his coat. 'I have to go out too,' he told me. 'I'll see you later, Watson.'

It was five o'clock when Holmes left. At six o'clock two men arrived with a large box which was full of food and drink. They prepared a table for five people and put the food and drink on it. They were following Holmes's orders, they told me.

Holmes returned at nine o'clock. 'They have brought the food, then,' he said.

'Who is coming?' I asked. 'There are five places at the table.'

'Yes. Lord Simon and two other people are coming. Someone is coming up the stairs now. That's probably Lord Simon.'

It was Lord Simon – and he looked very angry.

'You received my message, Lord Simon?' said Holmes.

'Yes, and I was very surprised. Are you sure about your facts?'

'Yes. I am quite sure.'

Lord Simon sat down and put his hands over his face. 'What will my father say?' he said sadly.

'It was an accident,' said Holmes.

'She has acted very badly,' said Lord Simon. 'What are people going to think? I shall never forgive her.'

There was the sound of a bell. Holmes went out and returned with a man and a woman. 'Lord Simon,' he said. 'This is Mr Frank Hay Moulton. You already know his wife.'

Lord Simon jumped from his chair. He was very angry. When the lady held out her hand, Lord Simon looked away.

'You are angry, Robert,' said the lady. 'I'm sorry.'

'You need not be sorry,' said Lord Simon.

'I have acted badly,' said the lady. 'I did not explain things to you. But when I saw Frank in the church, I forgot everything.'

'Perhaps Dr Watson and I should leave,' said Holmes.

Frank Moulton spoke for the first time. 'Please stay,' he said. 'I want everyone to know the complete story.'

'I'll tell you,' said the lady. 'I met Frank in California in 1881. My father was working on his claim. Frank and I fell in love and we wanted to marry. Then father found gold. It was a very rich claim. Frank had a claim too, but there was no gold in it. Father

63

Holmes went out and returned with a man and a woman.

grew richer as Frank grew poorer. I wanted to marry him, but my father refused to let me. He took me to San Francisco. Frank followed me there and we saw each other in secret. Frank decided to look for gold again. When he was rich, he planned to return. Before he left, we married secretly.

'Frank went to New Mexico and one day I saw a report in a newspaper. During an attack on a gold mine in New Mexico by Apache Indians, all the men at the mine were killed. There was a list of the men and Frank's name was there. After that I was ill for months. Then I met Lord Simon in San Francisco. Six months ago father brought me to London and I met Lord Simon again. He asked me to marry him and I agreed. Father was very pleased about the marriage. I loved Frank, but I thought he was dead.

'On the day of the wedding we went to the church. Frank was sitting there. He put his fingers to his lips and then wrote something on a piece of paper. I said nothing and the wedding continued. When I was leaving the church, I passed Frank. I dropped my flowers at his feet. He picked them up and gave them to me. With the flowers he gave me a note. It told me to join him later. I had to wait for a sign from him. I was married to Frank and I loved him. I had to follow him.

'We went back to the house, where I told Alice about Frank. I asked her to pack a bag for me. I told her not to tell anyone about it. I could not tell Lord Simon that I was already married. There were too many people there. So I decided to disappear. We sat down to eat, and through the window I could see the road and the park. I saw Frank. He looked at me and walked towards the park. I left the table and went upstairs. I put on my coat and followed Frank. A woman stopped me in the park. She said that Lord Simon was hers. It seems that Lord Simon also has a secret. I got away from the woman and found Frank. He took me to Gordon Square, where he had a room. He told me his story. The Apache Indians did catch him, and they held him for more than a year. But he got away from them and went to San Francisco. I was already in England so Frank followed me. He arrived in London on the day of my wedding.'

'I read about the wedding in the newspaper,' the American explained. 'It only gave the name of the church. It did not say where Hatty was living.'

'We had to decide what to do,' said the lady. 'Frank wanted to tell Lord Simon. But I just wanted to disappear. Later I planned to write to my father. Frank took my white dress, shoes and ring and threw them into the lake in the park. We were going to leave the country tomorrow. Then Mr Holmes found us. He said that I should tell Lord Simon. That is the complete story, Robert. Can you forgive me?' She held out her hand to Lord Simon.

'If it makes you feel any better,' he said, and took the lady's hand.

'And now,' said Holmes, 'will you all join me for dinner?'

'That is asking too much,' said Lord Simon. 'Now I shall say a very good night to you all.' He walked quickly out of the room.

'Mr and Mrs Moulton,' said Holmes, 'you will have dinner with me, won't you?'

They accepted.

After the Americans left, I said, 'Now Holmes, please explain. How did you know about Hatty Doran?'

'Well,' said Holmes, 'she went to church happy and came back unhappy. Something took place there. What was it? Lord Simon spoke of the man in the church. The lady dropped her flowers and he picked them up. So it was possible that he passed a note to her.

'When she came back from the church, she spoke to Alice. Lord Simon heard the words "jumping a claim". When Americans say that, it means taking something from someone. Lord Simon was taking Hatty Doran from another man and she was going to go away with that man.'

'How did you find them?' I asked.

'Lestrade showed me the note. On the back was the hotel bill. The man stayed at one of the best hotels in London. Only a few hotels have rooms at that kind of price. The note was from "F. H. M.", so I visited a few hotels. I looked at their books and I soon found the name Frank H. Moulton. He was an American. He was not at the hotel, but the hotel was sending his letters to 226 Gordon Square. I went there and found Mr Moulton at home. Hatty Doran was with him, of course. I suggested that they should see Lord Simon here. I told Lord Simon to come too. You saw the result.'

'Not a very good result,' I said. 'Lord Simon was not very kind to her.'

'Ah, Watson!' said Holmes. 'Put yourself in his place. He has lost a beautiful wife and a lot of money too. How easy do you think it is to be kind in his position?'

The Copper Beeches

One morning last spring I visited Sherlock Holmes. We were having some coffee when a visitor arrived. She was a pretty young woman. Her name was Violet Hunter.

'Please forgive me, Mr Holmes,' she said. 'I know that you are a busy man. But I would like your help with a rather strange situation.'

'Please sit down, Miss Hunter,' said Holmes. 'I shall be happy to help you. What can I do for you?' I could see that Holmes liked his visitor.

'I am a teacher,' she said. 'I worked for a Mr Munro for almost five years, teaching his children. But he went abroad two months ago and took the children with him. So I lost my job. I looked for a new one but I could not find one. I often visited an office in London which finds jobs for teachers. The business belongs to a woman called Miss Stoper. I went there once a week, but Miss Stoper did not have anything until last week. When I went in, a fat man was with her. He looked at me and turned to Miss Stoper.

'"This young woman is just right," he said. "Are you looking for a job?" he asked me.

'"Yes," I replied.

'"And how much do you want?"

'"In my last job I had four pounds a month," I said.

'"That isn't much," he cried. "If you come and teach my son, I'll pay you a hundred pounds a year."

'Well, Mr Holmes, I had no money and he was offering me a hundred pounds a year. It was a very good offer. He saw that I was surprised. Then he took some money from his pocket.

'"Here are fifty pounds," he said. "You probably need some

clothes. You can buy them with this."

'He seemed a very kind person, Mr Holmes. I had no money. I could not even buy food. But why was he giving me so much money? I decided to ask a few questions.

' "Where do you live, sir?" I asked.

' "In a house called the Copper Beeches. It is in the country, 5 miles from Winchester."

' "And what shall I have to do?"

' "I have a son who is six years old. You will look after him and teach him. My wife will sometimes ask you to do things. It won't be anything difficult. She will give you a dress and sometimes she will ask you to wear it. Will you do that?"

' "Of course," I agreed.

' "Sometimes she will ask you to sit near the window. Will you do that?"

' "Yes, I will."

' "And you will have to cut your hair short."

'As you can see, Mr Holmes,' said Violet Hunter, 'I have very long hair. I did not want to cut it short.

' "I am afraid not," I told him. "I don't like short hair."

' "But my wife does not like long hair," he said. "You will have to cut it."

' "No, sir, I do not want to cut it," I answered.

' "Then I can't give you the job," he said. "I'm sorry." He turned to Miss Stoper. "I would like to see some more of your young ladies."

'Miss Stoper was angry. "Do you want me to find you a job?" she asked.

' "Yes," I answered.

' "Why?" she said. "You have just refused a very good offer. Goodbye, Miss Hunter."

'Well, Mr Holmes, I returned to my rooms. I had no food and no money. Did I do the wrong thing, I asked myself? These people seemed rather strange, but they were going to pay me well. And what use was my hair? I can't buy food with my hair. Perhaps I was making a terrible mistake. The next day I received this letter from the same gentleman. I'll read it to you.

'THE COPPER BEECHES,

NEAR WINCHESTER.

Dear Miss Hunter,

Miss Stoper has given me your address. I have not yet found a teacher. Would you like the job? I can give you £120 a year and the work is not difficult. Sometimes my wife will ask you to wear a blue dress which belonged to my daughter, Alice. She lives in America now. She will also ask you to sit near the window sometimes. That isn't difficult, is it? But you will have to cut your hair short. I know that you would like to keep it; that is the reason that I am paying you so much. Please accept the job. I shall meet you at Winchester Station. Write and tell me the time of your train.

Yours truly,

JEPHRO RUCASTLE.'

'That is the letter, Mr Holmes. I would like to accept the job, but first I would like your help.'

'Well, Miss Hunter, you want the job, so you have to decide. I will say this. I would not want my sister to take the job. But you are not my sister. What do you think about Mr and Mrs Rucastle?'

'Well,' said Miss Hunter, 'Mr Rucastle seemed a kind person. I'm sure his wife is ill.'

'I think you are right,' said Holmes. 'It is not a job for a young lady.'

'But they will pay me very well, Mr Holmes.'

'Yes, too well. Why are they paying you a hundred and twenty pounds a year? They can find someone for forty pounds a year. There has to be a good reason.'

'I would like to take the job,' said Miss Hunter.

'Then take it,' said Holmes. 'If you are ever in danger . . .'

'Danger! Will it be dangerous?'

'I don't know,' said Holmes. 'But I will come at any time. Just send me a note if you need my help.'

'Thank you, Mr Holmes. I feel much happier now. I shall write to Mr Rucastle and I shall cut my hair tonight.' She said goodbye to us and left.

'What a nice young lady,' I said.

'Yes,' said Holmes, 'and we shall see her again very soon.'

Two weeks later, Holmes showed me a note from Winchester. It said: 'Please come to the Swan Hotel in Winchester at midday tomorrow. It is very important. Violet Hunter.'

'Will you come with me?' asked Holmes.

'Of course,' I said.

'There is a train at half past nine,' said Holmes. 'It arrives at Winchester at half past eleven.'

The next day we arrived in Winchester and went to the Swan Hotel. Miss Hunter was waiting for us there, and we all sat down to eat.

'I am so happy to see you,' she said. 'You are both very kind. I don't know what to do. I need your help.'

'What is it?' asked Holmes.

'I have to be quick,' she said. 'I need to get back before three o'clock. They are not unkind – it's nothing like that. But I am quite frightened. When I arrived, Mr Rucastle met me. We drove to his house, the Copper Beeches. It's a big square house. In front of the house there is a field which runs as far as the Southampton road. The road is 260 feet from the house. There are some copper beech trees in front of the house and they gave the house its name.

'Mr Rucastle was very nice to me and I met his wife and child. Mrs Rucastle is not ill, so we were wrong about that. She is a very quiet woman. She is Mr Rucastle's second wife. He also has a daughter from his first marriage. She is twenty and lives in America. She went to America because she did not like his second wife. That is what Mr Rucastle told me. Mr Rucastle is kind to his wife, but something is wrong. Mrs Rucastle is a sad woman and often cries.

'Two other people live at the house and work for the Rucastles. They are Mr and Mrs Toller. They are not very nice to me and I don't like them.

'For the first two days there was nothing unusual about my job. On the third day Mrs Rucastle came down for breakfast and said something to her husband. He came to me.

' "Miss Hunter," he said. "My wife wants you to wear a blue dress. There is one on the bed in your room. Will you go and put it on?"

'I found a light blue dress on my bed. The material was good but it was not new. It belonged to another woman. It fitted me very well, so I went downstairs. Mr and Mrs Rucastle were very pleased. We were in a room with a large window at the front of the house. There was a chair near the window and Mrs Rucastle asked me to sit in it. Then Mr Rucastle told me funny stories which made me laugh. But Mrs Rucastle did not laugh – she looked sad. Mr Rucastle told me funny stories for about an hour. Then suddenly he stopped and told me to change my dress.

'Two days later – the same thing. I wore the blue dress, sat near the window and Mr Rucastle told me funny stories. They made me laugh even more. Then he gave me a book and told me to read it to him. I read to him for ten minutes but suddenly he ordered me to stop. I was very surprised, because I was in the middle of a sentence.

'I always had to sit with my back to the window. Was

'Was something going on outside? I had an idea and the next day I hid
a small mirror in my hand.'

something going on outside? I had an idea and the next day I hid a small mirror in my hand. Mr Rucastle was telling his funny stories and I was laughing. I put my hand to my eyes and looked in the mirror. A man was standing on the road, looking at the house. He was a small man with a beard and he was wearing a grey suit. Then Mrs Rucastle saw the mirror.

' "Jephro," she said to her husband, "there is a man on the road, looking at Miss Hunter."

' "Is he a friend of yours, Miss Hunter?" asked Mr Rucastle.

' "No," I said. "I know nobody here."

' "Then give him a sign to go away."

'I did that. Then Mrs Rucastle told me to leave the room. That was a week ago. That is the last time that I wore the blue dress. It is also the last time that I saw the man on the road.'

'Are there any other strange things about the family or the house?' asked Holmes.

'Well,' continued Miss Hunter, 'there is a small building near the house. Mr Rucastle showed it to me. It has a small window.

' "Look in there," said Mr Rucastle.

'I looked inside and saw a very big black dog.

' "It's my dog, Carlo," Mr Rucastle told me. "He's very dangerous and only Mr Toller can do anything with him. Toller puts the dog in the garden every night. If anyone comes near the house, Carlo will kill them. Don't ever leave the house at night, Miss Hunter. The dog will kill you too."

'Then I made another discovery. One evening I was in my room, putting away my clothes. I was looking for places for them. The room was once Miss Rucastle's and I found some clothes. I think they were hers. Under the clothes I found a lot of hair. I thought it was mine – it looked the same colour. I kept my own hair after I cut it off. It was in my bag. I took it out and placed it next to the other hair. They were exactly the same colour.

'Then there is the top floor of the house. The rooms are not used. The Tollers live on the floor below and the door to the top floor is always shut. One day Mr Rucastle came out of this door, looking very angry. I went into the garden and looked at the windows on the top floor. One of them had boards against it. Mr Rucastle came into the garden.

' "What are you doing?" he asked.

' "I have just seen that window" I said. "It has boards against it."

' "Yes," said Mr Rucastle. "I take photographs and work on them in that room."

'I think he was lying, Mr Holmes. I wanted to see the room and yesterday that chance came. Toller and his wife were out with the boy. They forgot to shut the door to the top floor before they left. I went up the stairs. All the rooms were open except one. I tried to open the door but it was locked. Then I heard a noise in the room. Someone was in there. I was frightened and I ran down the stairs. Mr Rucastle was waiting angrily at the bottom.

' "What are you doing?" he asked.

' "I was looking round the house," I said. "It was so lonely up there that I was frightened."

' "Why do you think that this door is always shut?" he said.

' "I don't know."

' "To keep people out of there."

' "I did not know . . ."

' "Well, you know now. Don't ever go in there again," he shouted. "If you do, I'll throw you to the dog!"

'I ran to my room,' continued Miss Hunter. 'I was so afraid. I thought of you, Mr Holmes. I needed your help. I was afraid of the house, of Mr Rucastle and of the Tollers. I was free to return to London, but something was wrong in that house. What is the secret of the upstairs room? The nearest village is less than 2 miles from the house. I went there and sent you a letter. This morning I came here, but I have to go back before three o'clock. The

Rucastles are going to visit some friends. They will be there all evening and I have to look after the boy. What shall I do, Mr Holmes?'

Holmes stood up and walked about the room. 'Where will Mr Toller be this evening?' he asked.

'He will go to the village. He returns at about eight o'clock.'

'Good. The Rucastles will also be out of the house. That only leaves Mrs Toller. Is there a room under the house?'

'Yes,' said Miss Hunter.

'You are doing very well, Miss Hunter. Can you do one more thing?'

'I'll try. What is it?'

'Watson and I will come to the Copper Beeches at seven o'clock. Only Mrs Toller will be there. Ask her to get something from the room under the house and then shut her in.'

'I'll do it.'

'Very good, Miss Hunter. We shall soon know the secret of the upstairs room. I know one thing. They brought you here to take someone's place. That person is in the upstairs room.'

'Who is it, Mr Holmes?'

'I think it is Mr Rucastle's daughter, Alice. He says that she is in America. I think that he is lying. He chose you because you are like her. That hair you found is Alice's. It is the same colour as your hair. The man on the road is possibly Alice's friend, and perhaps he wants to marry her. They made you sit in the window with Alice's dress on while Mr Rucastle told you funny stories. You laughed a lot and Alice's friend could see this. Then they made you send him away. He probably thinks that Alice no longer likes him. He can't speak to her because the dog walks around the garden at night.'

'I think that you are right, Mr Holmes,' cried Miss Hunter. 'We have to help the poor girl.'

That evening we reached the Copper Beeches at seven

o'clock. Miss Hunter was waiting for us.

'Have you done it?' asked Holmes.

'Yes,' answered Miss Hunter. 'Mrs Toller is in the underground room and she can't open the door. Let's hurry – Mr Toller will be back soon.'

We went upstairs.

'This is the room,' said Miss Hunter. The door was shut.

'I hope that we are not too late,' said Holmes. 'I can't hear anyone in there. Help me, Watson.'

Together we pushed against the door and soon it was open. There was nobody in the room. There was a window in the roof, and it was open.

'Her father has taken her away,' said Holmes.

'But how?' asked Miss Hunter.

Holmes climbed on a table and looked through the window. 'There are some wooden steps resting against the roof,' he said.

'That's strange,' said Miss Hunter. 'They were not there when Mr Rucastle left.'

'Listen!' said Holmes. 'Someone is coming up the stairs. Perhaps it is Rucastle. You have your gun, Watson. Get ready. We don't know if he is dangerous.'

Mr Rucastle arrived at the door. He had a heavy stick in his hand. Sherlock Holmes ran towards him.

'Where is your daughter?' he said.

'I would like to ask you that question,' shouted Mr Rucastle. 'I have caught you. You'll be sorry!' He turned and ran down the stairs.

'He's gone to get the dog!' cried Miss Hunter.

'Let's shut the front door,' said Holmes.

We ran down the stairs. Then we heard the dog and there was a terrible cry. An old man came through a side door. It was Mr Toller.

'Help!' he cried. 'Someone has let the dog out. It's two days

77

Mr Rucastle was on the ground and the dog was standing over him.
It had its teeth in his neck.

since its last meal. Quick, or it will be too late!'

Holmes and I ran out of the house and saw the big black dog. Mr Rucastle was on the ground and the dog was standing over him. It had its teeth in his neck. I ran to the dog and shot it in the head. We carried Mr Rucastle into the house. He was very badly hurt.

A tall woman hurried into the room.

'Mrs Toller!' cried Miss Hunter.

'Mr Rucastle unlocked the door,' said Mrs Toller. 'Ah, miss, I knew about Miss Rucastle. Why didn't you ask me?'

'Ha!' said Holmes. 'Mrs Toller knows more about this than we do.'

'Yes, sir,' she said.

'Then tell us what you know,' said Holmes.

'Are the police coming?' said Mrs Toller.

'That is possible,' said Holmes.

'I helped Miss Alice,' she said. 'Tell the police that. She was never happy here. Then she met Mr Fowler and wanted to marry him. She had some money which her mother left her. She asked for her money but Mr Rucastle refused to give it to her. He was against her marriage because he wanted to keep her money. So he shut her in her room. This made her very ill and they had to cut her hair.

When she got better, she wanted to marry Mr Fowler as much as before.'

'So Mr Rucastle put her in that upstairs room,' said Holmes. 'He brought Miss Hunter from London and made her send Mr Fowler away.'

'That's right, sir,' said Mrs Toller.

'But Mr Fowler did not go away, because he loved Miss Rucastle. He spoke to you when you were in the village. He gave you money and you helped him.'

'Mr Fowler is a very nice man,' said Mrs Toller.

'You told him that your husband was going to the village tonight. You said that the Rucastles were also planning to be out.'

'That's right, sir. Then I put some wooden steps against the house.'

'Thank you, Mrs Toller. Ah, here's Mrs Rucastle. She has brought a doctor, so we can leave now, Watson. We will take Miss Hunter to Winchester. She can't stay here now.'

The mystery of the house with the copper beech trees was solved. I was able to save Mr Rucastle's life, but he was never completely well again. His daughter married Mr Fowler and is living happily with him in Australia. Holmes liked Violet Hunter very much. I hoped that his interest in her was going to continue. But when she was not at the centre of a mystery, he soon forgot her. She is now a well-loved teacher at a school in London.

ACTIVITIES

'A Scandal in Bohemia'

Before you read

1 Bohemia was the name of a country that does not exist now. Where
   was it? Look in books or on the Internet.
2 Discuss a famous fictional detective from TV, books or films. Why
   is he or she special or interesting?
3 Look at the Word List at the back of this book. Find:
   a words for professions.
   b titles for men from important European families.
   c things that a thief wants to steal.
   d subjects for an interesting news report.

While you read

4 Write the correct names. Who:
   a lives in rooms on Baker Street?   ....
   b travels in a beautiful carriage and   ....
          sometimes wears a mask?
   c is an American singer, born in 1858?   ....
   d plans to marry the King of Bohemia?   ....
   e lives at Briony Lodge?   ....
   f visits Briony Lodge every day?   ....
   g is the witness at a wedding in the Church   ....
          of St Monica?
   h throws a smoke bomb into Irene Adler's   ....
          sitting room?
   i keeps the photograph of Irene Adler in   ....
          evening dress?

After you read

5 The King of Bohemia says: 'I will give anything to get that
   photograph.'
   a Who has the photograph?
   b What does it show?
   c Why does he want it?
   d Does he get it by the end of the story?

6 Why does Sherlock Holmes dress as:

    a a driver?   **b** a priest?

7 Work with another student. Discuss the first two sentences of the story: 'Only one person ever beat Sherlock Holmes. Irene Adler was that person.' In what way did she beat him? How did she do it?

8 Imagine that you are one of these people. Explain why you are happy at the end of the story.

    a Irene Adler   **b** the King of Bohemia

'The Red-Headed League'

Before you read

9 The Red-Headed League is a group of people who all have red hair. Think of possible reasons for forming a group like this.

While you read

10 Number these in the correct order, 1–9

    a Sherlock Holmes, Dr Watson, Inspector Lestrade
       and Mr Merryweather hide behind boxes in an
       underground room in the City Bank.   .....

    b The Red-Headed League closes.   .....

    c Holmes and Watson go to a concert.   .....

    d Mr Spaulding shows his employer a piece from a
       newspaper.   .....

    e John Clay leaves the City Bank with Inspector
       Lestrade.   .....

    f Mr Wilson joins the Red-Headed League.   .....

    g Mr Wilson employs Vincent Spaulding.   .....

    h Mr Wilson starts working part-time in his shop.   .....

    i Holmes and Watson visit Mr Wilson's shop.   .....

After you read

11 Think about the crime that Sherlock Holmes wants to stop.

    a Why does Holmes spend the night in the underground room of the City Bank?

    b Who waits with him?

    c Who are the criminals?

    d Is the crime successful?

12 Work with another student.

  a Make a list of the facts that help Sherlock Holmes solve the mystery.

  b Discuss this question: What mistakes do John Clay (Vincent Spaulding) and Duncan Ross (William Morris) make?

'The Boscombe Lake Mystery'

Before you read

13 In this story the body of a man is found by a lake. What questions would the police and Sherlock Holmes like answers to? What do you think?

While you read

14 Are these sentences right (✓) or wrong (✗), or we don't know (?)?

  a Charles McCarthy and John Turner lived in Australia in the past. .....

  b McCarthy's wife and Turner's wife were good friends. .....

  c Boscombe Lake is many miles from McCarthy's house. .....

  d At least four people see McCarthy near Boscombe Lake on the day of his murder. .....

  e James McCarthy has a lot of friends in Bristol. .....

  f Charles McCarthy dies in his son's arms. .....

  g The two fathers want James and Alice to get married. .....

  h Mr Turner became ill in Australia. .....

  i Before his trip to Bristol, James McCarthy thinks that he is a married man. .....

  j Sherlock Holmes has met Mr Moran in the past. .....

  k Mr Turner explains Mr McCarthy's death to the police. .....

  l Holmes and Watson go to James and Alice's wedding. .....

15 Who are these people? Why are they important to the mystery?

    a John Turner   **d** Alice Turner

    b Charles McCarthy   **e** A young woman in Bristol

    c James McCarthy

16 What is important about these?

    a shoes with square toes   **d** *RAT*

    b a stone   **e** 'Cooee!'

    c a grey coat

17 When Holmes hears Turner's story, he promises: 'If the police free young McCarthy, it will stay a secret.' Why do you think that Holmes makes this promise?

'The Blue Diamond'

Before you read

18 This story is about an expensive diamond. The diamond is stolen. What other expensive things are often stolen? Do the police usually catch the thieves?

While you read

19 What are these people's jobs at the time of the story?

    a Peterson   ....

    b John Horner   ....

    c James Ryder   ....

    d Henry Baker   ....

    e Mr Windigate   ....

    f Mr Breckenridge   ....

    g Mr and Mrs Oakshott   ....

    h Catherine Cusack   ....

After you read

20 Explain what happens to the famous blue diamond. Start from the time when it leaves Lady Morcar, the owner.

21 Holmes discovers the complete story from James Ryder. Work with another student. Have this conversation.

Student A: You are Holmes. Ask questions until Ryder tells you everything. Start like this: *How did you know that Lady Morcar had a diamond?*

Student B: You are Ryder and you are very frightened. Answer Holmes's questions honestly. Then ask him not to go to the police.

'The Single Man'

Before you read

22 Read these lines from the story: 'Women often disappear before the wedding. They sometimes disappear a few days later. But the same day! That's very strange.'

a Do you agree with the speaker?

b What reasons do women (or men) have for disappearing: before a marriage?   after a marriage?

While you read

23 Who is it? Write **LS** for Lord Simon or **HD** for Hatty Doran.

a	the child of a poor English duke	.....
b	the child of a rich American gold miner	.....
c	more than forty years old	.....
d	less than thirty years old	.....
e	has a title and an older brother	.....
f	has a friend called Miss Flora Miller	.....
g	married another person	.....
h	has a friend called Alice	.....
i	looks old	.....
j	looks young and beautiful	.....
k	joins Holmes and Watson for dinner	.....
l	feels happy at the end of the story	.....
m	feels unhappy at the end of the story	.....

85

After you read

24 Complete the story.

Lord Simon, the son of ..**a**.., marries Miss Hatty Doran, the daughter of ..**b**.. . But Miss Doran is already married to ..**c**.., after she met him in ..**d**.. . She decides to marry again. She thinks that her first husband is ..**e**.. . She sees this first husband again at ..**f**.. . Later, she leaves her new home to join him. They throw ..**g**.. into a lake. They make plans to leave ..**h**.. . Then Sherlock Holmes finds them.

25 Work in pairs or groups and give your opinion.

    a Does Hatty Doran do the right thing?

    b Is Lord Simon right to be angry with her?

    c Is Sherlock Holmes very clever to solve the mystery? Or is it quite simple?

'The Copper Beeches'

Before you read

26 In mystery stories from the 1800s, a person often disappears. Sometimes the person is dead, and sometimes the person is hidden by his or her enemies. Why do you think a writer has a hidden person or body in a story? How can this make the story more interesting or more frightening?

While you read

27 Circle the correct words.

    a Violet Hunter is *rich/ poor* and has *a good job/ no job*.

    b Mr Jephro Rucastle will pay *a little money/ a lot of money* for a teacher for *his son/ his daughter*.

    c The teacher has to have *long/ short* hair and sometimes has to wear a *blue/ black* dress.

    d Sherlock Holmes thinks that the job at Copper Beeches will be *dangerous/ enjoyable* for Miss Hunter.

    e Mrs Rucastle is Mr Rucastle's *first/ second* wife. She *is/ isn't* ill and she *is/ isn't* often sad.

    f Violet Hunter has to sit near a *door/ window* and listen to Mr Rucastle's *funny/ sad* stories.

g Violet sees a *small / tall* man in a *blue / grey* suit on the road.

h Carlo is *the friendly gardener / a dangerous dog* at Copper Beeches.

i Violet discovers a lot of hair. It is very *similar to / different from* her own hair. She also discovers a room with a *locked / open* door, and she hears *nice music / a frightening noise* in the room.

j Sherlock Holmes and Miss Hunter believe that *the first Mrs Rucastle / Alice Rucastle* is in the upstairs room.

k Carlo almost kills *Mr Rucastle / Mr Fowler*.

l Alice escapes from Copper Beeches. She marries *Mr Toller / Mr Fowler* and moves to *Australia / America*.

After you read

28 Work with another student. What do you know about the lives of these people before, during and after the story?

    a Miss Violet Hunter   **d** Miss Alice Rucastle

    b Mr Jephro Rucastle   **e** Mr Fowler

    c The second Mrs Rucastle   **f** Mr and Mrs Toller

29 Tell the story in your own words from the time when Holmes and Watson arrive at the Copper Beeches.

Writing

30 You are the King of Bohemia and are now unhappily married to the King of Scandinavia's daughter. Write a letter to Irene Adler (now Mrs Norton) about your sad life.

31 It is fifteen years after the deaths of Charles McCarthy and John Turner. Write a conversation between Alice and James McCarthy and their children. One of the children can begin the conversation like this: 'Mother and Father, please tell us about our grandparents.'

32 You are Alice Rucastle (now Mrs Fowler) and are living in Australia. You want to forgive your father and visit him on your next trip to England. Write a letter to him.

33 How did Holmes solve the mystery? Choose one of the stories and explain.

34 You are one of the people who were helped by Sherlock Holmes. Write a letter thanking him for his help. Tell him what you are doing now.

35 'In these stories, Sherlock Holmes seems to prefer the women to the men.' Do you agree?

36 Sherlock Holmes is often kind to the criminals that he catches. Do you think this is right? Why does he act like this?

37 Write a conversation between Dr Watson and his wife. Mrs Watson wants to know more about Sherlock Holmes. Why is the great detective so interesting to her husband?

38 Why are the Sherlock Holmes stories so popular, do you think?

39 You are in trouble. Imagine what your problem is. Write a letter to Sherlock Holmes. Explain your problem and ask for his help.

Answers for the Activities in this book are available from the Penguin Readers website. A free Activity Worksheet is also available from the website. Activity Worksheets are part of the Penguin Teacher Support Programme, which also includes Progress Tests and Graded Reader Guidelines. For more information, please visit: www.penguinreaders.com.